THE WAKE OF
WELLINGTON

THE WAKE OF
WELLINGTON

Englishness in 1852

Peter W. Sinnema

Ohio University Press
Athens

Ohio University Press, Athens, Ohio 45701
www.ohio.edu/oupress
© 2006 by Ohio University Press

Printed in the United States of America

Ohio University Press books are printed on acid-free paper ⊗ ™

14 13 12 11 10 09 08 07 06   5 4 3 2 1

Jacket art: Wellington's death mask, by George Gammon Adams,
1852. © National Portrait Gallery, London. Frontispiece: *Last Moments of
the Duke of Wellington, Illustrated London News,* 12 November 1852 (detail).

Library of Congress Cataloging-in-Publication Data
Sinnema, Peter W.
 The wake of Wellington : Englishness in 1852 / Peter W. Sinnema.
   p. cm.
 Includes bibliographical references (p.   ) and index.
 ISBN 0-8214-1679-0 (acid-free paper)
  1. Wellington, Arthur Wellesley, Duke of, 1769–1852—Death and burial.
 2. Funeral rites and ceremonies—Great Britain—History—19th century.
 3. Wellington, Arthur Wellesley, Duke of, 1769–1852—Influence. 4. National
characteristics, English—History—19th century. 5. England—Civilization—
19th century. I. Title.
  DA68.12.W4S56 2006
  941.07092—dc22
                              2005027742

In the ordinary course of things, a century hence there will still be some score old people in this country who will talk to incredulous hearers of the Duke of Wellington's funeral; and in the year 2000, A.D., there will be a few score more who will relate what their own fathers told them about it.

—*Times* (London), 19 November 1852

CONTENTS

ILLUSTRATIONS

ACKNOWLEDGMENTS

The idea for this book originated in 1995 when I took up a postdoctoral fellowship at Birkbeck College, University of London, with funding from the Social Sciences and Humanities Research Council of Canada; the council has been generous with subsequent support in the form of a standard research grant with attached teaching release stipend. The Departments of English and Faculties of Arts at York University and the University of Alberta have been equally charitable in fostering my research. I am particularly grateful to past departmental chairs—Maurice Elliot, Kim Ian Michasiw, and Jo-Ann Wallace—who went out of their way to encourage and facilitate my work. Chris Woolgar kindly arranged my visiting fellowship at the Hartley Institute, University of Southampton, and the staff at the British Library, the Newspaper Library, Colindale, and Rutherford Library, University of Alberta, were invariably courteous and helpful. The Royal Hospital, Chelsea, deserves special mention for supplying the image of Wellington's lying in state, as does Marcie Whitecotton-Carroll for preparing the picture for my use. The photographers at Robarts Library, University of Toronto, and at the University of Alberta's Creative Services did an excellent job in producing many of the other illustrations.

Jim Ellis has been my most assiduous reader and an unfailing friend during writing. Laurel Brake, Graham Dawson, Robert Appleford, Mark Simpson, and Ian Munro have also earned my gratitude by reading bits and pieces of the manuscript. Several friends and colleagues with interests in things Victorian—Susan Hamilton, Monica Flegel, Lauren Gillingham, Christine Ferguson, and Carmen Ellison—have been catalysts for my work in important ways. George Barrow and Cath Geale were munificent London hosts and genuine benefactors on various occasions. David Sanders, Nancy Basmajian, and the editorial staff of Ohio University Press have been a true pleasure to work with; to the press's anonymous readers must go much of the credit for anything that is really good in the following pages. Janet Wesselius has been my intellectual and emotional constant throughout, and Alynne Sinnema came along halfway through to make everything so much more fun: I dedicate this book to the two of them.

Earlier versions of chapters 4, 5, and 7 have appeared, respectively, in *Nineteenth-Century Prose* 26, no. 1 (1999): 142–68; *Victorian Review* 25, no. 2 (2000): 30–60; and the *Oxford Art Journal* 27, no. 2 (2004): 219–38.

INTRODUCTION

This is a book about the First Duke of Wellington's posthumous symbolization as a rallying sign for the English nation. It examines the duke's legacy as it was constructed, amplified, defended, and contested in Britain in and after 1852, the year of his death and his extraordinary state funeral. I am not interested in writing another *True Book about Wellington*,[1] reconstructing a subject whose as yet neglected biographical features wait in the margins of or at the interstices between the extant publications and manuscripts. Rather, I want to annotate what might be called the "Wellington effect," the way in which the heroic individual's eminence was persistently identified with national destiny.

Such a project inevitably confronts Wellington's fundamentally typological composition. The dead duke was repeatedly caught up in interpretive practices that stressed the quasi-symbolic relations between hero and nation. This hermeneutic system, in turn, invariably took the form of progressive revelation or what George Landow has called a "secularized figuralism."[2] Wellington could serve, according to rhetorical exigencies, as either a type or the antitype—either a deliverer of Europe from Napoleon's predations and hence an anticipation of the Continent's permanent release from the threat of French republicanism or the replete embodiment of an unsullied Englishness that had been prefigured in earlier, less illustrious soldier-heroes. In both cases, Victorian polemicists at midcentury consistently distinguished Wellington as the chief agent in an analogical scheme that construed national history, in the words of A. C. Charity, as a process of ongoing "'prefiguration' and 'fulfilment.'"[3]

Ultimately, Wellington's spectacular funeral pageant was a threshold event against which his life could be re-viewed and comprehended as the consummation of a national destiny intimately bound up with Englishness itself, with what it meant to be English in the middle of the nineteenth century. If there was any validity to the declaration made by the *Times* (London) shortly after his death that Wellington "was the very type and model of an Englishman,"[4] then his funeral could also mark the end, as Cornelia Pearsall has suggested, "not of just a great Englishman, but, more troublingly, of the last one, as if with him [went] the epitome of the national type."[5] How this particular affinity between Wellington and Englishness was forged and came to be pervasively imprinted on the national consciousness, especially in the early months after the hero's death, is the subject matter of my book.

As a result of this focus on the multivalent afterlife of Wellington, my approach is synchronically interventionist rather than diachronically ordered. Readers looking for a sequential account of Wellington's life will probably be disappointed; those with little or no knowledge of his biography are referred to the following chronology as a point of entry into a study whose goal is to survey a cross section of texts and images in order to discuss how certain representations of the hero contributed to a nation's self-imagining.

My terrain is therefore constituted not so much by the readily available biographical material as by what the London-based *Examiner* of 1852 called the "Wellington literature," a corpus that the event of the hero's death, in particular,

> suddenly called forth [and that] . . . extended into every department
> of writing . . . marked by every degree of intellectual merit. It . . . com-
> prised short articles of every quality, singular for ability or singular for
> the absence of it, in newspapers, reviews, and magazines; orations in
> the senate, original or stolen; sermons out of all pulpits, from cathe-
> dral to meeting house; histories, new or reprinted, varying in literary
> merit over an exceedingly wide range; and poems of all ranks, from
> the Ode of Tennyson down to the Dirge of Tupper.[6]

The *Examiner*'s mildly caustic assessment of the Wellington tributes, figured as indifferent literary effluvia motivated by the vanity and greed of their authors, reflected this periodical's long-standing political opposition to the High Tory duke. But the newspaper also put into focus the material *The Wake of Wellington* sets out to canvass: a profuse and, for some time after 1852, a dramatically proliferating Wellingtoniana.

One mid-Victorian biographer recognized that death itself generated a renewed interest in Wellington, a sudden reawakening of pride in national achievement that appeared to be unprecedented:

> Multitudes of the young, who had not become familiar with Wellington's history, wished to become familiar with it now; multitudes of the old who had been contemporaneous with it, wished now to read it in regular form. . . . Authors, artists, publishers, and miscellaneous venders could scarcely supply the market quickly enough for the popular demand. All sorts of Wellingtoniana, literary and artistic, historical and curious, old and new, great and small, were in peremptory request. . . . In short . . . emphatically and almost in the style of hero-worship, Wellington was "the topic of the day."[7]

By the time he published his influential two-volume biography near the end of the nineteenth century, Herbert Maxwell was able to claim that "it is hardly possible to open a book dealing with civil, military, or social affairs in England . . . without finding constant allusion to Wellington."[8]

The way in which the hero was laid to rest had much to do with the creation of an insatiable Wellington market. As the London and provincial papers tried to impress upon their readers, the duke's death was celebrated on a spectacular, unprecedented level. His state-sanctioned funeral took two months to prepare and drew more than one and a half million spectators to London. In the following pages, I consider the cultural repercussions of this funeral—how they were registered in that constellation of posthumous representations that seemed consciously driven to transfix Wellington into a revered, indeed an unequaled national hero for the mid-Victorians. If this "fixing" had its inaugural moments in Wellington's early successes on the battlefields of India and western Europe, it had its most extraordinary instantiation in the public spectacle of the duke's funeral on 18 November 1852, which laid to rest the man one eulogist called England's "incomparable Hero and Patriot" with "a ceremony that surpassed all former sepulchral grandeur," causing "all the sensibilities of human nature [to rise] to a wonderful height of melancholy rapture."[9] According to another contemporary observer, the nation could "fairly assert that there is no precedent at all for the celebration of the funeral worth consulting, simply because there is no precedent in our history of the life or death of such a hero—of so great and good a man."[10]

I adopt three senses of the term *wake* as I interrogate these claims about the unrivaled nature of Wellington's heroic distinction, in the process drawing out the various meanings implicit in my title. Most obviously, I employ the word to denote a vigil that simultaneously deplores and hallows the passing of a hero whose "manners . . . opinions . . . aspirations . . . [and] prejudices, seem to have been wholly English."[11] Hence, *wake* also implies a requiem of sorts for the English, left behind to witness and mourn the passing of an exceptional incarnation of themselves. As the *Oxford English Dictionary* notes, the word *wake* derives in part from the ecclesiastical Latin *vigilia,* or certain feast days preceded by services lasting through the night, and so encompasses the idea of festivity or making holiday. Wellington's wake was certainly an occasion for ostentation and circumstance; one cleric regretted "the burying of his corpse with empty pomp, and noisy, griefless, sorrowless, selfish parade."[12] Rather than dwell on the authenticity or hubris of the celebrants' grief, however, I would like to maintain a distinction: instead of attempting to retrieve that which, in the end, is inaccessible and unverifiable—the actual emotional states of mourners lining London's streets or crowded into St. Paul's Cathedral— I am concerned with the ways in which a self-described community of mourners was transformed by spectacle.

This distinction leads to a second sense of *wake:* the track left by a passing, a path of disturbance. Differentiating between the natural body (the corpse) and the social body (the permanent commemorative image left behind in iconography, memorial, or effigy), Nigel Llewellyn has noted that "funerals of the great were . . . deeply memorable occasions which helped construct and reconstruct the complex patterns of social experience." Public mourning, according to Llewellyn, "was almost totally concerned with signifying practice rather than with psychological therapy. . . . [During] the death ritual the natural body was virtually forgotten and culture's concern was to support the accumulation of meanings attributed to the social body."[13] Focusing primarily on that liminal period of approximately two months between Wellington's expiration and funeral, when the public and its representatives accustomed themselves to a hero's death and prepared for his final departure by planning appropriate observances, this book taps into that "accumulation of meanings" ascribed to the duke's social body.

One way in which that body could be represented, for example, is shown in the special masthead for an *Illustrated London News* (*ILN*) supplement (18 September 1852), wherein the duke appears in the guise of a Roman potentate, his aged and withered frame made virile, his neck made muscular, his pointed jaw squared, and his notoriously beaked nose made elegantly aquiline (figure 0.1). This Romanized, laureled Wellington, whose cameo is surrounded by the instruments and emblems of war, is a striking amelioration of the effigy as it appeared in a camera lucida sketch by the sculptor Thomas Milnes, who was granted access to the corpse shortly after Wellington's death (figure 0.2). It is also far from reminiscent of the toothless and haggard face imprinted for posterity in the death mask (figure 0.3). The Wellington of the *ILN* masthead instead demonstrates that such relics of moribundity were part of a large and diverse commemorative practice that ranged from the production of gaunt mementos mori to the aggressive promotion of what Frank Turner has called the "Victorian cult of Julius Caesar."[14] "There was in [the Duke's] features," the *Leeds Mercury* claimed on the same day the *ILN* supplement appeared, "a character something of the stamp of the ancient Roman: his bust might be placed between the old bronze head of Junius Brutus and that of the first Caesar of the Capital, without being challenged as out of place."[15] If Victorian Britain appropriated classical models because it saw affinities between its own imperial objectives and those of its supposed cultural forebears, the Victorian funeral looked back as effortlessly as it searched for ideals of heroic masculinity.[16]

Wake, of course, also has a third meaning: the act of awakening. Anyone familiar with British military or political history will know that Wellington's name does not need to be roused from obscurity. Indeed, "any author who undertakes to add yet another book to the corpus of Wellingtonian literature, vast as it is, may justly feel that he has a need . . . to account for his temerity."[17] It is my comparatively modest goal to wake Wellington from the torpor of the conventional biographical lore that has

FIGURE 0.1 Special masthead, *Illustrated London News*, "Life of the Duke of Wellington" supplement, 18 September 1852.

FIGURE 0.2 *The Duke of Wellington, after Death*, camera lucida sketch by Thomas Milnes, 1857. © National Portrait Gallery, London.

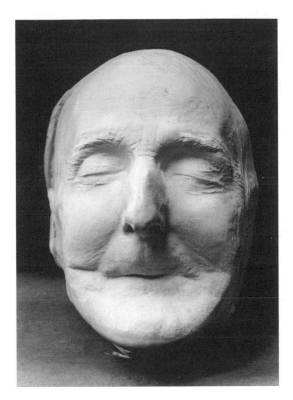

FIGURE 0.3 Wellington's death mask, by George Gammon Adams, 1852. © National Portrait Gallery, London.

enshrined him within a narrative "straight line" that invariably attempts to show how the duke "had worked his way up from the lowest reaches of the Irish peerage by a combination of talent and influence."[18] The question to be asked, then, is not "Who was Wellington?" but "What purposes did Wellington serve?" How was Wellington's story told and retold, and what significance did the Victorians invest in these different rehearsals of renown or infamy?

These stories were particularly multifarious in late 1852. Whereas clergymen set about sanctifying Wellington's elaborate funeral by arguing that "rites suited to the age, rank, station and character of the departed, are not displeasing to God, nor contrary to his holy word,"[19] poets indulged their theatrical inclinations in an attempt to adequately describe the occasion. The miscellaneous writer Nicholas Michell was especially expansive:

A Nation, like one man, seems here,
A Nation comes to drop a tear,
A Nation sighs above the bier—
O Death! Is this thy prey? . . .
  Words fail to paint the scene whose glory
Excites the land, shall live in story;
It awes the mind, and dazzles sense,
Gloom striving with magnificence.
Wealth, art, and power combine to throw
A halo 'round our cloud of woe;
  A world seems met—all-glorious sight—
To honour this great funeral rite.[20]

  Given such hyperbole, it is perhaps not surprising that Wellington's funeral has often been maligned by cultural and literary historians as the cynosure of outlandish ritual, as "the high point of Victorian funeral extravagance," or as a "fine example of the Victorian exhibition of funerary display taken to extremes of redundancy."[21]

  Recently, though, more sustained and less dismissive attention has been given to the organization and cultural aftereffects of the funeral. In an essay on the "immortal" Wellington, Neville Thompson provides a schematic survey of some of the stylized lamentations that helped to perpetuate prevailing romantic ideas about the death of heroes.[22] Iain Pears discusses antithetical representations of Napoleon and Wellington, offering some important insights into Wellington worship and patriotism at midcentury.[23] John Wolffe devotes a chapter specifically to Wellington's funeral in his book on grieving, religion, and nationhood in Britain, tracing in some detail the convoluted involvement of many different agencies in the funeral preparations and the reactions of those many spectators who were stirred by "a wish to observe a grand spectacle and to participate in an historic community and national event."[24] And in an article cited earlier that seeks to explain the Victorians' "extravagant desire for proximity to [Wellington's] remains," Cornelia Pearsall poses a question that resonates with the present study's central interest in the hero's cultural afterlife: "What *can* these remnants . . . all of the products spawned in the wake of one man's death . . . tell us about Victorian culture?"[25]

The scope of all four investigations into "what it was to be English" in the wake of Wellington, however, is quite severely limited; the studies do not satisfactorily flesh out the modes and meanings of Wellington's postmortem reconstruction and modification, even as they establish conclusively that the funeral was "a public spectacle of an unprecedented and unmatched character."[26] As initiatory explorations of Wellington's procession and obsequies, they bespeak a rich site of meaning that deserves further scrutiny, suggesting that the duke's death gives present-day observers a chance to study an instance of Victorian self-display and, within the dramatically condensed time frame of a few months, Victorian self-fashioning.

More sustained exploration along these lines has, indeed, been undertaken since the mid-1990s, but Wellington has fallen outside its purview. The life and times of Queen Victoria, for example, have been meticulously reassessed by scholars such as Adrienne Munich and Gail Turley Houston, who attempt to situate their prominent subject within a larger "web of cultural forces that were conflictual, simultaneous, and always in process."[27] These scholars have done much to uncover and illuminate the often contradictory interpretations of Victoria's cultural images in order to understand what different people, to use Munich's phrase, "make of their given world."[28] Stephen Behrendt also deserves special mention for his conscientious examination in *Royal Mourning and Regency Culture* of the "person, events, artifacts and public culture that intersected in the event of Princess Charlotte's death" on 6 November 1817. "What these intersections reveal about how culture functions," Behrendt argues persuasively through an analysis of the literary and extraliterary artifacts produced to commemorate the princess, "can tell us much about the perennial attraction of private and public mythmaking."[29] The theatrically mourned Charlotte provides a superlative illustration of the ways in which historical figures come to be invested with qualities of myth, qualities that conflate the personal and the public or domestic and national interests.

Whereas Victoria and Charlotte have been critically engaged as both complex figures and "ideas" accommodated by Victorian culture "to represent its self-interested moment,"[30] Wellington remains predominantly tied to the biographical subgenre of the male, British, military hero, notable for its quest for historical authority and its drive toward a certain type of untainted purity, within and yet largely isolated from cultural practice. It is precisely as a challenge to this conventional narrative that a prolonged case study of the duke through the lens of death commends itself.

Of course, the nineteenth century witnessed numerous imposing funerals. Horatio Nelson, William Pitt, and Charles James Fox, for example, had all been buried with ceremony in 1806. Nelson's body was borne on a miniature wheeled version of the *Victory,* the ship he commanded at Cape Trafalgar, through the streets of London before being lowered into a vault in St. Paul's Cathedral—a well-staged, allegorical production of the vice admiral's last journey that was to be carefully studied and in several ways mimicked by those responsible for Wellington's procession and the design of his ornate funeral car.[31] Richard Sheridan, the impoverished Irish dramatist, was honored with a magnificent Westminster Abbey funeral in 1816, and George Canning was buried near him in a state ceremony some eleven years later. William Gladstone's 1898 funeral—other than Wellington's, the only post-1806 instance of an officially public funeral for a nonroyal personage (that is, a funeral requiring prior parliamentary resolution)[32]—saw the great statesman's body conveyed by special train from Hawarden to London, where three hundred thousand people passed by his catafalque in Westminster Hall in the two days preceding a burial service that, in its solemn grandeur, was widely thought to have been "an authentic expression of the national mood."[33]

Only the queen's funeral, however, can be said to vie with Wellington's for the depth of its symbolism, although the transportation of Victoria's body early in 1901 from Osborne House to London by royal yacht and private train was intentionally designed to produce an aura of circumspection rather than make a public statement about the passing of the nation's "mother." Whereas Victoria's funeral "has become part of the English saga, for people saw in her passing the end of their own way of life,"[34] Wellington's death was construed as the definitive consummation of the Napoleonic era, at least as it had been experienced and represented in Britain. Although clearly both an extension and a perpetuation of the lionizing biographies that had found their inspiration in the duke ever since he cleared the French out of Portugal and Spain between 1808 and

1814, the posthumous Wellington literature developed distinctive "Victorian" characteristics, reflective of the social, political, and historical scene of the 1850s. I attempt to gain some purchase on this distinctiveness and to outline its contours by reading "the literature" through the public celebration of the military hero's death in seven chapters.

Chapter 1 outlines the chief contours of Wellington's allusiveness—the ways in which he kept turning up or leaving traces of himself in genres as various as the novel, the newspaper, the biography, and the memoir. A brief consideration of representative texts from these genres demonstrates their contribution to an iterative process whereby the duke's reputation was framed and promoted through the repetition of increasingly formulaic anecdotes and allusions. Chapters 2 and 3 follow analogous paths of inquiry, suggesting that Wellington's funeral was a portentous affair, anticipated in unique ways by other "national" events and modes of heroic representation. Chapter 2 revisits the Great Exhibition of 1851, that much analyzed gathering of nations, as an occasion from which Wellington's funeral took its measure. Chapter 3 traces the discursive consolidation of three exceptional traits in the dead Wellington: simplicity of character, common sense, and the veneration of duty. Wellington's death by natural causes at Walmer Castle in Essex, a comparatively unpretentious edifice of the Cinque Ports, came to be seen as an eminently suitable demise for a man widely regarded to be the pattern of candid austerity.

Chapter 4 inquires into the sorts of opportunities and anxieties that arise when a state funeral is, by necessity, postponed for a significant period of time. A bewildering array of artworks and commemorative objects relating to Wellington were produced and sold between September and November 1852. Postmortem mementos revitalized the duke's reputation, but they also raised questions about which images and relics most faithfully represented Wellington. The chapter traces a shift, marked primarily by the press, away from initial anxieties about crowd control to a retrospective reading of participants' good behavior as an armistice between classes. Chapter 5 focuses on the procession and burial, attending in particular to the perceived aesthetic success or failure of both. Although it was ultimately sanctified by Prime Minister Edward Stanley, Earl of Derby as a stellar example of "perfect organization" and "admirable arrangements," the funeral attracted a range of contentious responses in its immediate aftermath, from indiscriminate acclaim to hostile revulsion. The chapter considers the various, often contradictory effects the public spectacle had on observers, and it closes with a look at the ways in which various clergymen exonerated the gorgeous procession from possible charges of secular excess.

Chapter 6 reads Wellington through and against the fractious Irish press in an attempt to account for the various counterdiscourses that threatened from the margins of the seemingly unanimous, positive legacy of the war hero. Typically, the detractors expressed their aversion to the Wellington worship from outside England, downplaying the "real importance of the subject" of Wellington's death by astringently remarking that obsessive coverage of the event resulted from "the dearth of other topics susceptible of being written about."[35] Chapter 7 serves as a fitting epilogue, taking up once again Wellington's "incarnation" of the nation's blood in order to explain the 1883 banishment from Hyde Park Corner of Matthew Cotes Wyatt's colossal equestrian statue of the duke. This chapter chronicles a sculptural travesty, but it also argues that, as an expression of the "industrial sublime," Wyatt's statue failed to correspond with the most popular image of Wellington as the nation's dutiful servant. In the frustration of sublime ambition that resulted in the statue's rather unceremonious removal, we witness an important debate about the nature and form of public commemoration.

What follows, then, is a study of an exemplary life not as the linear unfolding of an "assured and evolving career"[36] but as it can be read through and after the fundamentally transmogrifying event of death. This approach reads Wellington "backwards": reading for and through the vitality of his death at the advanced age of eighty-three, against the flow of that Victorian biographical tradition wherein "the vacillations and discontinuities of character are . . . resolved through the secular structures of aims, motivations, drives, pursuits, vocations, directions and meliorations —in short, 'rise, progress, improvement.'"[37] As I have noted with regard to recent considerations of Queen Victoria's and Princess Charlotte's legacies, this tradition has been challenged by scholarship that encourages students of the Victorian era to engage in radical and unapologetic adaptations of seemingly stable cultural texts. A self-conscious practice of adaptation offers an alternative to the heroic portraits of moral rectitude whose most prevalent form, Martin Stannard notes, is the "two-volume eulogy, designed to assist with our fathers' decorum at the lying-in-state of our great men."[38] The risk of falling back into an ingenuous duplication of either the form or the credos of the decorous eulogy is attenuated once "we agree to see that those who read . . . are in fact always 'after' and always 'aftering,' always restoring, adapting, supplying, making texts and promulgating meanings."[39]

The Wake of Wellington is such an exercise in "aftering": interpreting and providing a critical framework for what followed after Wellington, from a historical point that comes well past that initial period of posthumous after-ness. In the case of Wellington, I approach death and its celebration as the initial moments that inaugurated after-ness, opening up the floodgates of possibility for an enormous variety of ideologically inflected eulogizing. To read the celebration of death in these terms is to complicate the more self-evident claim that "life becomes transparent against the background of death, and fundamental social and cultural issues are revealed."[40]

A CHRONOLOGY OF
THE DUKE OF WELLINGTON

1769 Born as Arthur Wesley in Dublin, 1 May (?), to Garret Wesley and Anne Hill, Earl and Countess of Mornington; Napoleon born in Ajaccio, France

1781 At Eton (until 1784)

1786 At the Académie Royale d'Equitation at Angers, France

1787 Assigned as ensign to the 73rd Foot Regiment; promoted to lieutenant in December

1790 Elected to the Irish parliament as member for the borough of Trim (until 1795); made captain in June

1793 France declares war against England; Wesley promoted to major in April, lieutenant-colonel in September

1794 Participates in abortive campaign at Ostend against the French

1796 Embarks for India, arrives at Calcutta in February 1797; promoted to colonel; Napoleon made commander of the army of Italy

1797 Older brother Richard, Earl of Mornington, made governor-general of India and adopts orthography of "Wellesley," as does Arthur

1798 Richard arrives in India; Napoleon defeats the Mamluks in Egypt

1799 First Mahratta War—Wellesley invades Mysore; siege of Seringa-patam, which ends with death of Tipoo Sultan on 4 May; Napoleon's coup d'état in Paris and nomination to first consul

1800 Catches and executes Dhoondiah Waugh

1802 Second Mahratta War—Wellesley fights against Peshwa of Poona and Scindiah of Gwalior; promoted to major-general

1803 Ahmednuggur captured by Wellesley's forces; Battle of Assaye, 12 August; Battle of Arguam, 29 November; siege of Gawlighur ends 15 December

1804 Made knight companion of the Bath; Napoleon assumes title of emperor

1805 Meets Horatio Nelson at the Colonial Office in London; death of Nelson at Trafalgar

1806	Marries Catherine "Kitty" Packenham; elected member of Parliament for Rye (until 1809)
1807	Made chief secretary of Ireland by Duke of Richmond; successfully captures Danish fleet
1808	Arrives in Portugal, 24 July; British troops arrive in force, 1 August; Battle of Rolica, 17 August, initiates the peninsular war; Battle of Vimeiro, 21 August; Convention of Cintra, 22 August; returns briefly to England on 4 October
1809	Makes last visit to Ireland; crosses the Douro River and liberates Oporto; Battle of Talavera, 27 July
1811	Battle of Fuentes, 3 May; Wellesley made general and knight, Grand Cross of the Tower and Sword
1812	Lays siege to Badajoz; Salamanca surrenders, 27 June; Battle of Salamanca, 22 July; victoriously enters Madrid, 12 August; Parliament makes him a marquess and grants him £100,000; inducted into Order of the Golden Fleece
1813	Napoleon retreats from Russia; Battle of Vitoria, 21 June, which results in King Joseph Bonaparte's defeat and Wellesley's promotion to field marshal; siege of Pamplona, which falls 28 July; San Sebastian raised, 31 August; crosses the River Bidassoa into France, 7 October; Battle of the Nivelle, 10 November; made knight of the Garter
1814	Takes Toulouse, 10 March; Napoleon abdicates and is exiled to Elba; Wellesley returns to Dover, 23 June, is made Duke of Wellington, and joins House of Lords, 28 June; takes up diplomatic post as ambassador in Paris; meets Mme. Anne-Louise-Germaine de Staël; Lawrence paints the first of four Wellington portraits, *The Duke As He Appeared on the Day of Thanksgiving at St. Paul's*
1815	Joins Congress of Vienna in February; Napoleon escapes Elba in March; Battle of Quatre Bras, 16 June; Battle of Waterloo, 18 June; Napoleon exiled to St. Helena; Wellington made commander in chief of the allied armies of occupation and rewarded with Strathfieldsaye
1816	Bombing of Wellington's mansion in Paris; Lawrence paints untitled Wellington portrait for Charles Arbuthnot
1817	Returns from duties as ambassador to France; purchases Apsley House, London

1818	Allied armies vacate France; Wellington joins Liverpool's government as master-general of the ordnance; Lawrence paints two Wellington portraits, *The Duke on Horseback* and an untitled canvas for Robert Peel
1820	Death of George III; Wellington negotiates with Queen Caroline on George IV's behalf; pro-Caroline mob unhorses Wellington in London
1821	Death of Napoleon; death of Caroline
1822	Richard Westmacott's *Achilles* statue erected in Hyde Park
1825	Publication of Harriette Wilson's *Memoirs;* Wellington travels to Russia to mediate peace between the Russians, Turks, and Greeks
1826	Made constable of the Tower
1827	Made commander in chief and colonel of the Grenadier Guards; death of George Canning
1828	Becomes prime minister, 15 February (until November 1830)
1829	Peel and Wellington form the Metropolitan Police; Wellington made lord warden of the Cinque Ports and inherits Walmer Castle
1829	Wellington's ministry passes the Catholic Relief Bill in February; Wellington fights duel with Earl of Winchilsea
1830	Death of George IV; Wellington speaks against Earl Grey's and Earl Russell's reform measures in the House of Lords, 2 November
1831	Kitty dies, 25 April; Apsley House attacked and windows smashed, 27 April; Wellington's horse and carriage attacked on London streets
1832	Reform Bill passed, 7 June
1834	Wellington's second ministry begins, 12 November (until Peel takes over later in the same month); made chancellor of the University of Oxford and secretary of state for foreign affairs
1837	Death of William IV; Victoria becomes queen
1839	Colonel John Gurwood publishes the twelfth and final volume of Wellington's *Dispatches* (begun in 1834)
1840	Napoleon's body removed from St. Helena and transferred to Les Invalides in Paris

1841   Joins Peel's government as minister without portfolio

1844   Francis Chantrey's equestrian statue erected outside the Royal Exchange, London

1846   Retires from public life, resigning as leader of the Opposition for the House of Lords; Matthew Cotes Wyatt's equestrian statue erected on Burton's Arch at Hyde Park Corner

1848   Made lord high constable of England; organizes military defense of London against Chartists

1850   Made ranger of Hyde Park and St. James's Park

1852   Dies at Walmer Castle, Essex, 14 September; body removed to London, 10 November; public lying in state at Chelsea Hospital, 13–17 November; procession and funeral at St. Paul's Cathedral, 18 November; Alfred, Lord Tennyson publishes *Ode on the Death of the Duke of Wellington*

1857   Publication of Thomas Hughes's *Tom Brown's School Days*

1861   Completion of the Wellington obelisk in Phoenix Park, Dublin

1875   Completion of Wellington's canopied tomb in St. Paul's

1883   Wyatt's Wellington statue removed to Aldershot

THE WAKE OF
WELLINGTON

ONE

Aftereffects

Wellington and Englishness

WELLINGTON'S death diversified considerably the field of possibilities for imaginative investments in him. As Graham Dawson has observed, the death of military heroes in the nineteenth century inevitably resulted in a proliferation of ennobling narratives in which their deeds "were invested with the new significance of serving the country and glorifying its name. Their stories became myths of nationhood itself, providing a cultural focus around which the national community could cohere."[1] The cogency of this double process of national investment and myth-making depended, in large measure, on its articulation within a familiar typological framework, wherein the dead hero could be associated paradigmatically with national hopes and aspirations. In turn, its hegemony could be guaranteed only through the habitual exclusion of narratives that conflicted with the national hero's sanitized image, with his demonstrated worthiness as a subject for public veneration.

An examination of Wellington's discursive constitution in the posthumous literature can therefore begin with Thomas Hughes's best-selling work of fiction, *Tom Brown's School Days* (1857), a text that negotiates an exemplary type upon which the students of Rugby could pattern themselves. Hughes's novel undertakes an analogical exercise, borrowing the concepts popularly used to describe one ideal character—the indomitable Wellington of Waterloo—for the description of another—the morally and physically robust public-school boy. This chapter sets *Tom Brown's* apparently spontaneous assimilation of the Wellington legend alongside similar acts of deification in eulogies in the *Illustrated London News,* the *Times,* and Herbert Maxwell's important *Life of Wellington.* It closes with some reflections on the politics of omission with reference to Harriette Wilson's scurrilous, invariably neglected *Memoirs* of 1825. The ways in which these authors exhume and enhance the legend of Wellington as, in Maxwell's words, modern history's "dominant personality"—and the ways in which they, in turn, are taken up or assiduously ignored by other writers—provide us with useful insights into the process of mythmaking itself.

Long celebrated as Victorian fiction's quintessential celebration of English manliness-in-embryo, *Tom Brown's School Days* is a prominent voice within what Herbert Sussman has called the competition among multiple possibilities for male gender formation.[2] The novel is broadly acclaimed for making an important contribution to the philosophy of muscular Christianity, "the interrelated development of the individual's physical and spiritual strength,"[3] and it reads like a direct response to James Anthony Froude's famous challenge to British authors to produce a particular breed of historical novel, "plain broad narratives of substantial facts, which rival legend in interest and grandeur."[4] Hughes's narrator, himself "a devout Brown-worshiper" and an enthusiastic Old Boy, praises the Rugby prefect system developed under headmaster Thomas Arnold in the 1830s, which rigorously prepared students for what Hughes calls "yeoman's work"—able leadership at home and bold defense of empire abroad.[5] As numerous critics of the novel have demonstrated, Arnold's Rugby rapidly gained prominence in the Victorian imagination as an "unsurpassed institution of man-making" thanks to Hughes's nostalgic reminiscences about his own years as a public-school boy.[6]

Tom Brown's School Days, however, is of particular interest in the context of the present study for its occasional references to the Napoleonic

era. Published almost half a century after Napoleon's final defeat at Waterloo, Hughes's novel repeatedly represents public-school life as "a battlefield ordained from of old." Arnold, a "tall, gallant form" with a "kindling
eye," is viewed by Brown's comrades as a "fellow-soldier and the captain
of their band." A schoolhouse football match elicits battlefield imagery
reminiscent of the nation's victory against the French in Belgium: "Reckless
of the defense of their own goal, on they [the opposing house team] came
. . . straight for our goal, like the column of the Old Guard up the slope
at Waterloo." After winning the match, Tom and his chums indulge in a
night's singing. "The Siege of Seringapatam," commemorating the young
Colonel Wellesley's first great military success in India, is chorused rous-
ingly. Throughout, Hughes's narrator interjects his own moral lessons,
enjoining male readers to "play your games and do your work manfully."[7]

Wellington and his army function as a familiar, exemplary subtext in
this injunction. They provide an inspirational and historical model for
manliness, the developmental apotheosis of "boyishness," or "animal life
in its fullest measure, good nature and honest impulses."[8] The all-male
world of Rugby finds in the Napoleonic past a pattern for self-disciplined,
energetic, productive manhood.[9] Evidently, another subtext in Hughes's
novel is a remark popularly attributed to Wellington that the Battle of
Waterloo was won on the playing fields of Eton, the duke's own alma
mater.[10] Given *Tom Brown*'s central tenet that "the object of all schools is
. . . to make . . . good English boys, good future citizens,"[11] allusions to the
"Wellington of Eton" who eventually became the incomparable Wellington of Waterloo connote a potent medley of highly serviceable meanings:
heroism, integrity, and rugged masculinity, fostered in the dormitories and
on the grounds of the public school, could find no better paragon for emulation than the man one anonymous panegyrist called "The lion-heart, and
eagle-eye— / The Pride of England's chivalry."[12]

These allusions say something important about the operations of cultural memory and the possibilities for historical representation in the wake
of Wellington—but they are hardly surprising. Norman Vance explains
them in terms of the author's personal experience: "Tom Hughes's life-
long interest in the navy and in the armies which defeated Napoleon I was
prompted by the reminiscences of his elders,"[13] those who had actually

lived through the years of French-English conflict between 1793 and 1815, roughly the period of Wellington's active military service. In this interpretation, the exploits of Wellington and the British army on the battlefields of India, the Iberian Peninsula, and western Europe are a predictable, familial inheritance, the stuff of generational gossip and hence natural reference points for mid-Victorian nationalists such as Hughes.

Hughes's use of battle imagery to portray the rough-and-tumble of Rugby sport, however, can be understood culturally as well as psychologically. Hughes engages with the Napoleonic past and various of its dramatis personae as self-evident narrative tools efficacious in the promotion of "pluck and hardihood and the spirit of fellowship and co-operation in the school house."[14] In mid-Victorian Britain—and Hughes's novel about the militaristic training of "manly and honest" boys illustrates this point nicely—the recently dead Wellington served much the same role as "King Shakespeare" in the third chapter of that bible of Victorian manliness, *On Heroes, Hero-Worship and the Heroic in History*. Thomas Carlyle's pantheon of dead heroes, published in 1841, was not ready to receive into its fold the still very much alive duke, although the author noted, on various occasions in his diaries, his admiration for the elderly Wellington, "truly a beautiful old man . . . [with] an expression of graceful simplicity, veracity, and nobleness."[15] Along with Carlyle, however, Hughes's readers might pose the rhetorical question, "Does not [Wellington] shine, in crowned sovereignty, over us all, as the noblest, gentlest, yet strongest of rallying-signs; *indestructible*; really more valuable in that point of view than any other means or appliance whatsoever?"[16]

In the 1850s, as *Tom Brown's School Days* suggests, the answer would have been a resounding yes. If Carlyle had been speaking of Wellington rather than Shakespeare, his words could not have more aptly expressed a sentiment common among Britons at midcentury: "This [Wellington] is ours; we produced him . . . we are of one blood and kind with him."[17] To read Wellington as a sign capable of rallying national fervor through a process of reciprocal identification, however, is also to attribute to the *idea* of Wellington a certain stability. If the hero was to be interpreted broadly as one of Carlyle's indestructible appliances, a "tangibly-useful possession" of England,[18] then his legacy had to be anchored in a generally acceptable and accepted narrative that explained who Wellington was and how he was to be received. Such fixing was only really possible once he was dead; the coherence lent to such heroes was felt to be particularly acute during the funerals themselves, which functioned as occasions for the invigoration of individual reputation and for the generation of new heroic narratives.

In Wellington's case, the period just before and after the funeral saw a widespread and intensive investment of national qualities in the duke—virtually "every writer projected onto the Duke of Wellington the demanding ideals of the age and saw in him the perfect hero in Victorian dress: selflessly devoted to the interests of his country; modest and heedless of rewards, honours and display; diligent and meticulously attentive to detail; patient and punctual, temperate and thrifty."[19] Such is the heavily weighted duke Hughes uses as a reference point for the moral development of Tom and his chums, and the process of attribution is typological in nature: Wellington's life provides Hughes with an intelligible (because self-evident) formal pattern for evolving male patriotism and citizenship.

Concomitantly, Hughes's reference to this immediately recognizable secular type has valuable effect for the writer. As George Landow has demonstrated, the interpretive habits of most literate Victorians were heavily influenced by typology, a result of the way that sermons, religious tracts, hymns, and commentaries—especially those of an evangelical persuasion—trained them to read their Bibles. Biblical reading practices of the typological variety, in turn, were gradually popularized as an appropriate interpretive paradigm for secular texts. The seemingly arcane theological matter of typology, wherein God is seen to have placed anticipations of Christ in the laws, events, and people of the Old Testament, increasingly influenced secular thought as the nineteenth century progressed. Hughes's Wellington, therefore, permits the author "to communicate with his audience in terms of a recognizable, culturally acceptable narrative or structure which has many powerful associations attached to it."[20] Those associations —national devotion, patience, punctuality, thrift—position the duke as the very type of English rectitude that readers could both identify with and emulate. Wellington is thus caught up in what Jane Tomkins calls the Victorians' "eschatological vision": he is situated as the chief protagonist in a narrative that reenacts secularly the sacred drama of redemption.[21]

This point about the typological composition of Wellington's posthumous representations deserves further elaboration. It can be made more apparent by considering how the duke was discursively fashioned as a pattern for English valor in genres other than fiction. To this end, we might take a momentary look back to a historical concurrence that predated *Tom Brown*'s publication by five years. Wellington's death itself had taken on added drama and meaning by coinciding roughly with Louis Napoleon Bonaparte's assumption of the title Napoleon III in Paris. The younger Bonaparte's audacity contributed significantly to the Wellington mythology by enabling a reassertion of a strand of retrospective interpretation that had been largely forgotten in the post-Waterloo years—Wellington's divine preordination as Napoleon's nemesis. The ambitions and demands of the so-called *partie impérialiste,* or imperialist party, with its amplified calls for a revival of the glories of the Napoleonic era, raised the specter of renewed French aggression just when Britain was laying its last great peninsular war hero to rest: "Authors of all stripes linked the death of the English hero and the resurrection of the French one through his nephew as a possibly ominous sign for the future."[22]

Paranoia about the declaration of empire in December 1852, therefore, compounded with a marked escalation of time-honored comparisons of Wellington with Napoleon. As Iain Pears has noted, "The contrast between [Wellington] and Napoleon Bonaparte was an enduring element in contemporary literature."[23] The antithesis of personalities was most often elaborated in narratives that opened with a comment on the serendipity of shared birth years: "The year 1769 witnessed several glorious births; but certainly there was nothing more remarkable in that year than the simultaneous appearance on the stage of the world of the two men who were to meet at Waterloo. It appears that Providence proposed to balance one by the other." Typically, they concluded with a moral, drawn from a comparison of Wellington's prolonged and distinguished political career with Napoleon's rapid decline as a failed outcast on St. Helena: "Is not such a lesson a striking proof of the final ascendancy of reason and of good sense over all the boldness and the flights of imagination and genius?"[24]

In turn, the reinvigoration of analogical language after the duke's death sought to concretely differentiate Englishness from an insidious French character at a time of apparent crisis. French political intrigues of the early 1850s reminded Britons of Napoleon's "soaring genius and insatiable ambition," whereas Wellington could be recalled as a model of "devotion to public service" and "commonsensical genius."[25] Ultimately, Wellington was widely declared to be a supreme exemplar of motivations and actions that were "honest, magnanimous, truthful, honourable and kindly"; Napoleon, "treacherous, disloyal, amoral, a cheat, a liar and a bully,"[26] was his "natural" foil. Casting its inimitably acerbic eye on such distinctions, the Edinburgh-based newspaper, the *Scotsman,* highlighted their constitution and perpetuation in narrative rather than in nature, playing with the doctrine of "natural" attributes by noting that the "contrast between the characters of Wellington and Napoleon, is naturally forced upon every reader of history. . . . [I]t has supplied and to the end of time will continue to supply multitudes of writers with admirable materials for antithetical composition."[27]

Whereas Karl Marx lampooned the 1851 coup d'état as a cynical "conjur[ing] up [of] the spirits of the past," a borrowing of "names, battle slogans and costumes in order to present the new scene of world history in . . . time-honoured disguise,"[28] *Punch* ridiculed Louis Bonaparte's imperial pretensions by representing the newly minted emperor as a freshly hatched chicken, applauded by an adoring audience of stick figures (figure 1.1). Many Britons, however, were unable to dilute their anxieties with satire. In his singularly apocalyptical sermon at London's Bethesda Free Chapel in honor of the recently deceased Wellington, Arthur Augustus Rees warned his congregation of the "new" Napoleon's ambitions, retracing the history of his uncle's destruction as a portent of the contemporary crisis: "All physical barriers being removed in the manner I have explained, the way to the empire seemed pretty clear [for Louis Bonaparte]; but one moral impediment stood right across the road, viz., the presence of the conqueror of Napoleon—the victor of Waterloo—the Iron Duke. Alas!

FIGURE 1.1. *All but Hatched! Punch*, 16 October 1852.

That barrier is now swept away; and Napoleon rises again in full stature, in the person of his nephew. . . . The beast itself revives."[29]

Punch added a postscript to this rather astonishing oratory two days after Wellington's funeral in a column entitled "The Duke's Last Honours." "May existing peace be ever unbroken!" exclaimed London's self-styled *Charivari,* "but now, when Liberty over all Europe is extinct, what would not Continental despots and bigots give to tread out its fire conserved and still blazing in this little island? It was well and judicious to advertise to them and the world with what enthusiasm we yet honour military heroism."[30] This well-rehearsed rivalry indicates the importance of the funeral as an affair that reinvigorated ongoing English and French political antagonisms through a collective remembrance of the Napoleonic era. Wellington's postmortem image was to be "fine-tuned to suit the requirements of an industrial but hierarchic society . . . deeply alarmed at the implications of France's revolutionary legacy."[31] More important, the funeral set the stage for subsequent interpretive endeavors to link Wellington's career with national providence. Just as Arthur Wesley's birth signaled the promise of Europe's emancipation from French tyranny, with Waterloo serving as the fulfillment of that peculiar covenant, so the "event-structures" that made up British Napoleonic history attained "continuity or interaction" through this symbolic pairing with the "national" hero's life.[32]

Wellington's funeral itself, then, required a scripted rhetoric that effected a postmortem transference of the duke's floridly enumerated attributes onto the nation in whose name he fought and governed. Through this rhetoric, Carlylean, manly heroism was located in the deceased duke and ultimately reinvested in England, to become an essential part of that nation's cultural and ideological composition.[33] If *Tom Brown's School Days* stands out for its imaginative transference of Wellingtonian virtue onto Rugby's students, effectively turning the dead hero into a transcendent exemplar for English boys on the playing field and in the dormitory, newspapers were equally energetic in their attempts to consecrate Wellington as both a symbol of the national psyche and a model for compatriots. Advocating a lavish ceremony for the duke, the *Illustrated London News* alleged that "England owes this great funeral, not so much to Wellington, whose fame it cannot enhance, as to itself"; the day after the funeral, another London paper, the *Globe and Traveller,* was satisfied that "the Nation [had] honoured itself in Wellington."[34] The duke exercised a permanent impact in the way his character gradually became sutured to the essential fabric of Englishness.

One need look no further than the *Times,* that "mouthpiece of public opinion . . . and most influential of [nineteenth-century] newspapers,"[35] to get some sense of how the Victorian press insisted on proclaiming Wellington's thorough embodiment of Englishness. In a lead column that was to be heavily plagiarized by numerous other periodicals in the coming weeks, the *Times* articulated a typological relationship between the exemplary individual and a national ideal, borrowing one concept (that of the "great man") to describe another (the consummate Englishman): "Indeed, all of us, though ever so far or ever so near,—if any were near him in the race of honour,—have felt only pleasure in the reflection that we had so great a man in our age and our country; and, more than all, that the man thus ours by the accident of birth was, to the very heart's core, and the very marrow of his bones—an Englishman."[36] There is much to unpack in such a passage, but at this point, I shall only touch upon one or two of its most pertinent features. The *Times* itself was far from transparent and perhaps far from certain about the precise meaning of the concepts with which it engaged. Yet it is clear that the vocabulary employed assumed and to some extent enjoyed a reciprocal understanding between writer and readers in 1852. Whatever "an Englishman" may have been in the context of this tributary essay—and it will be imperative to grapple with this complex issue—it was obviously meant to summon exclusively positive connotations in the mind of the implied reader.[37]

Earlier *Times* columns had mentioned the duke's "manly, compact, and clear" career and his "energy and public virtue,"[38] desirable attributes in a model Englishman. And it is this role of modeling that must be emphasized, for, along with Hughes, the *Times* was primarily interested in promoting Wellington as an exemplar. English mourners were asked to see something of their best selves, of that ineffable, national *something* they all shared, in the much lamented duke. In this sense, the newspaper was simply a more sophisticated version of Marie Maurice's portrait of Wellington's life, published in 1853 for the moral benefit of "young persons." The dedication to Maurice's didactic *Historical Sketch* defined Wellington-ian Englishness, offering a useful template through which the *Times* can be read: "Dedicated to the children of Great Britain, with the earnest hope, that the bright example held up before them, in the consistent loyalty, the single-minded patriotism, the faithful devotedness to duty, and the steadfast love of truth, manifested throughout the long life of Arthur, Duke of Wellington, may lead them to emulate his virtues, and to tread in his steps."[39] Loyalty, patriotism, duty, and truthfulness thus coalesced in the ideal Englishman. But even more telling than these positive attributes in the definition of this commendable type were those properties consistently execrated as being un-English and unmanly. In the nineteenth century, as David Morse has argued, to be English was to *not be* myriad others and other things. Englishness, as he puts it, "means to be English, as against Irish, Scottish, or Welsh, to be Saxon rather than Celt; it designates the interests of the aristocracy and the middle class, which have to be defended against the workers; it means having property and 'a stake in society'; it is also to be Anglican rather than a Catholic or a Dissenter; to be male rather than female; to be law-abiding and opposed to violence; it is to be respectable and contented rather than disreputable and discontented."[40]

The Wellington with whom English mourners were asked to identify at the funeral and in most of the posthumous literature was therefore not simply the virtuous man of patriotic duty and devotion to the Crown but also the blue-blooded, unpretending, antirevolutionary, decidedly un-Celtic hero whose birth to Anglo-Irish peers in Dublin did nothing to prevent the *Times* from insisting on his being English "to the very heart's core."

Wellington's death ceremonies functioned, then, as a specular exchange. Spectators conferred upon the duke the distinction of embodying perfectly a rather abstract but highly cherished set of "English" attributes; in turn, as a collective unified by their Englishness, they could aspire toward achieving, if less completely, those ideals to which they were naturally inclined by virtue of their national and racial heritage. "In paying tribute to the man they thought they knew so well," Neville Thompson has observed, "the Victorians were able to indulge their enjoyment of the celebration of death and mourning and honor themselves in hailing the individual who more than any other had been the very embodiment of work and duty."[41]

As an opportunity for specular self-gratification, Wellington's funeral also contributed to the historical prominence of its staging ground, London. Subsequent chapters are fairly meticulous in their description of the funeral as a metropolitan event, but at this point, it is worth emphasizing that Wellington memorialization was a national (and nationalist) industry. James Curl identifies a "cult of memorials" peculiar to the age of empire that "achieved great impetus in the nineteenth century. . . . [E]very new war brought forth patriotic memorials. Nationalism therefore was a most important factor in the development of memorials . . . [that] bear witness to a glorification of arms and a new overweening national pride."[42] Wellington's lying in state at Chelsea Hospital and the procession through Westminster and the City bound together the concept of a national-cultural memory with the significance of spatial representation. The funeral, in other words, stamped itself indelibly in the capital's social memory precisely through its spatial staging: it came to be perceived as a profound episode in the history of London, in the ideological construction of that metropolis as the world's economic and cultural capital during the early Victorian era. Celebration of Wellington's legacy, therefore, transmogri-fied into a celebration of the English themselves, of the city in which they congregated, and of the nation that had produced their hero. The procession's route along Pall Mall and the Strand and up Ludgate Hill gave occasion for artists and commentators to commemorate some of the city's most significant buildings—to "sell" London to readers as a global center of commerce, wealth, and prestige.

The *Illustrated London News*, for example, devoted more than one hundred full pages of print and high-quality wood-block engraving to Wellington between September and November 1852. The death and funeral were good news for this pioneer of regularly illustrated journalism, which saw its sales rise dramatically as a result of its innovative coverage of the funeral only ten years after it was founded.[43] It also tried to awe its readers with a description of the uncommon social cathexis that dignified the city's and nation's dead center on 18 November, St. Paul's Cathedral. There, the lowering of Wellington's coffin through the floor directly beneath the dome to rest permanently beside the remains of Horatio Nelson finished off a full day of patriotic service and ardor—and gave the paper a chance to take a competitive swipe at Catholicism in the years immediately following the so-called papal aggression: "Nearly 20,000 people assembled in St. Paul's. . . . The great cathedral of Protestant Europe embraced within the shadow of its mighty dome the rank, genius, learning, eloquence, wisdom, valour, and enterprise of a nation unsurpassed for arts, arms, and dominion. Its Princes, judges, priests, senators, warriors, merchants, heralds, were here marshaled in picturesque and glittering splendour around the tent of a hero."[44]

This remarkable passage provides insight into the figurative importance of the funeral as a painstakingly conceived, elaborately dramatized event that put London, its grandees, and its institutions at center stage along with Wellington. Its extraordinary linguistic concatenation suggests that this historic instance of "sepulchral idolatry"[45] was enormously satisfying to mourners gathered at the interment: they participated in an act of self-veneration, Wellington's corpse serving as the lodestone that brought together emissaries of the legal, commercial, academic, political, religious, and military vocations who genuflected before their own representative, "picturesque and glittering splendour." Wellington's final role was quite literally to "marshal" the nation's most illustrious delegates, the model of an Englishman summoning ancillary national types, so that the duke's commemoration was ultimately the affirmation of "a nation unsurpassed for arts, arms, and dominion."

If Wellington's death celebrations staged Englishness, London, and the nation, they also provided the ideological portal through which many of the biographers were to examine the duke and his times. The typical Wellington biography after 1852 attempted to establish for posterity the image of a hero whose death complemented euphoniously the tenor of his life. Thus, the *Morning Herald* of London declared:"Full of years as of honour, with eye undimmed and natural force unabated, the Great Captain has been as happy in the mode of his death as in the details of his career. He has been reserved for a calm and almost painless extinction; and Death has laid his hand lightly upon one who has been singularly exempt, throughout life, from the common weaknesses and sorrows of humanity."[46] This strain of memorializing was to culminate in Herbert Maxwell's monumental *Life of Wellington* (1899), which set a standard for balanced analysis and disinterestedness.

Maxwell's book also acknowledged an ulterior, more ambitious goal, however, signaled by its subtitle, *The Restoration of the Martial Power of Great Britain.* "I shall esteem myself fortunate," Maxwell notes in the preface, "if I have succeeded in placing the action of George III's Ministers in a truer light."[47] Maxwell's recuperation of Georgian reputations would probably have encountered some resistance earlier in the century, when the excesses of the prince regent and his court were being increasingly denounced by defenders of moral restraint and respectability, the latter perhaps the leading virtue of the Victorian age. Recovery and defense, however, are executed with a consistently moderate tone, since Maxwell finds "few things . . . more wearisome than unstinted panegyric." Instead of vaunting homage, he points to Wellington's funeral as the most estimable testament to the duke's "life so full of accomplishment . . . [and] service so long and devoted," a ceremony through which that life can be read and to which nothing needs to be added by way of commentary: "There [was] never an occasion which justified the most ample tribute of praise of a public servant and of mourning for his loss."[48]

Conspicuous for its restrained style, evoking a spirit of piety seeking primarily to improve and elevate its readers rather than to entertain or even inform them, Maxwell's long-awaited "impartial judgment pronounced on [the duke's] character"[49] typifies the prevalent biographical tradition of the nineteenth century. Valued as neutral, free from the contamination of authorial bias, and representing itself "as one of the last strongholds of empirical knowledge,"[50] this tradition finds an eloquent defense in the *Life*, which relentlessly portrays Wellington as a master of self-regulation and possessor of an inflexible will, traits that guarantee personal success and, indeed, determine European history. Repeatedly, readers are reminded that the future duke's early habits and experiences laid the groundwork for an inevitably distinguished military and political career. As representative for the borough of Trim in the Irish parliament of 1787, for example, Arthur Wesley (as he was known at the time) "acquired the habit of private study, without which his mind never could have been furnished to deal effectively with the vast variety of work it was applied to in after years." Arriving in Calcutta early in 1797, the young colonel immediately displayed the "zeal and success with which, in every subsequent enterprise, he grappled with and overcame . . . difficulties." By the end of the peninsular campaign in 1814, "this steadfast spirit maintained its purpose, this vigilant brain converted every changing circumstance to its use. . . . Calm, confident, resourceful, [Wellington] went from strength to strength, till Europe began to recognize her true deliverer."[51]

Maxwell's narration of Wellington's military career is filtered through these occasional, proleptic observations. Although not particularly noteworthy in themselves, they constitute a familiar element of biography, which relies on various techniques of anachronism to produce narrative cohesion and meaning. Taken in their aggregate, however, the effect of such iterative anticipations—in which the reader is allowed to see one of Wellington's personal attributes as a necessary catalyst, the first in a series of ever more admirable virtues that lead to imminent renown—is more interesting. They imply inevitability, itself an integral component of the Wellington myth as it was narrated from the time of his death. As one scholar has noted, foreshadowing "can suggest a sense of fatalism, or predestination . . . [so that] we can only watch the progression towards the final result."[52] This progression has already been touched upon as a central feature of Victorian typological biography. Maxwell works unquestioningly under its imperative, echoing Carlyle's view that "Universal History . . . is at bottom the History of . . . Great Men"[53] in his own reflection that "History, when written, seems to be composed of the acts of a few public men."[54] As a Great Man, one of Carlyle's "messengers," "sent from the Infinite Unknown,"[55] Wellington is an agent of destiny: his vocation and his triumph, especially as the destroyer of Napoleon, are in essence foreordained.

But this sublime role can only be recognized and confidently attributed to the hero once he has successfully completed his mission, only after the fact. And, as I have suggested, the biggest fact in this retrospective assessment is always death, which clears the way for "representations . . . [that] seek strategies to stabilize the body . . . transforming it into a monument, an enduring stone. Stable object, stable meanings: the surviving subject appropriates death's power in his monuments to the dead."[56] Death allowed commentators well before Maxwell to suggest, often much more explicitly, that Wellington was indeed "sent" as a deliverer and should be monumentalized as such. More than one Anglican clergyman proclaimed on the duke's death that, to quote to C. R. Alford, "God, in his wise providence, [had] raised [Wellington] up at the commencement of this century to give, not to Britain only, but to Europe and the world, deliverance from one of the most unscrupulous and unprincipled oppressors. . . . He appears an instrument specially raised up and qualified by God for the work He called him to perform. . . . We clearly trace in his history the Providence of God."[57]

Here again, Wellington is inserted into the now familiar typological narrative of prefiguration, wherein the circumstance of his birth presents itself as the promise or confirmation of another momentous event, "deliverance." This mode of commemoration reads modern European history teleologically, through its realization in the mighty acts of Wellington.

Although Maxwell appears to accept a modified and somewhat secularized version of this instrumental reading, portraying Wellington as a hero whose unique aptitudes guaranteed his success and fame, his restoration project laments the fact that the "truer light" it resolves to shed on Wellington must also illuminate the dark corners of posthumous mythmaking: "From the earliest times foremost men have become after death the subjects of manifold myth, and stories of every degree of mendacity were sure to gather round such a dominant personality as Wellington."[58] Maxwell's history, in contrast, works deliberately to demythologize (and concomitantly idolize) its subject by sticking to a chronological presentation of what Froude called "substantial facts," those that "appear to rest on trustworthy evidence."[59] An imperative for *The Life of Wellington* is to uncover more about and hence penetrate more deeply into the "real" subject, constituted by an exceptional past, singular influences, and a continually developing psyche leaving traces of itself in writings, deeds, and, perhaps more dubiously, the anecdotal memories of others.

Ultimately, Maxwell's *Life* can be understood as a superb specimen of what Edmund Gosse called "the big-biography habit" through which "we in England bury our dead under the monstrous catafalque of two volumes (crown octavo)."[60] The *Life* stands as a monument to the narrative process of purification, free of sex, scandal, and self-doubt, a heroic portrait of moral rectitude. Acts of exclusion, as my language here suggests, are every bit as important to this process as positive testimonies to heroic virtue. The idealized Wellington of Maxwell's *Life* is as much the product of narrative omissions and exculpations as he is of insistent praise; the authorized and authoritative version of Wellington that emerges is one exorcized of any hint of peccadillo. Through postmortem sanitization, the duke is made into a suitable Victorian gentleman and a candidate for national homage.

A brief look at one expunged episode in Wellington's past—Harriette Wilson's derisive profile of the great duke in her infamous *Memoirs*, resolutely ignored as a source text in Maxwell's retrospective—illustrates that any citation of her risqué diaries would jeopardize, would indeed be anathema to Maxwell's testamentary act. To ask why Wilson is neither quoted nor alluded to in the *Life* is to address the ideological presuppositions that govern the sayable in the wake of Wellington. Along with other "stories of mendacity," Wilson's *Memoirs* are relegated to the trash heap of history as Maxwell censures the "manifold myth" attached to Wellington.

Certainly, Maxwell could not have been unaware of the *Memoirs*. Wilson was one of the most notorious English courtesans of the late Georgian period, mistress to the Earl of Craven at age fifteen and over time the well-paid paramour of Wellington, the Duke of Leinster, Lord Hertford, Marquis (Richard) Wellesley, the Earl of Fife, Lord Gower, Beau Brummell, Viscount Ponsonby, and Lord Byron, among others. Her *Memoirs* went through thirty editions in 1825 alone, causing such a sensation that "Stockdale's [Wilson's first publisher's] door was thronged ten deep on the mornings announced for the publication of a new volume."[61] Although her lack of specificity, along with a "loose and slipshod style [that] does no credit to the editor,"[62] made Wilson vulnerable to charges of gross fabrication, the appearance of her "slight sketches" caused widespread consternation among those great men the author felt "ought to be exposed." If most of Wilson's victims defiantly refused to be blackmailed into paying for the author's silence (Stockdale's advance publicity had been accompanied by an invitation to defamed subjects to pay for the suppression of the *Memoirs*), their reputations suffered nonetheless as the reading public eagerly consumed the tales of sexual and political intrigue.[63]

In the *Memoirs*, the younger duke comes off very badly indeed.[64] Wilson is unashamed of her profession, but she alleges that she "will be the mere instrument of pleasure to no man. He must make a friend and companion of me, or he will lose me."[65] Wellington's complete inability to entertain Wilson intellectually, let alone satisfy her sexually, is evident from their first meeting. From the outset, then, his failure as a lover, as well as his conversational ineptitude, is underwritten by his obvious mental and physical inadequacies. Wilson's contempt is reserved primarily for Wellington's double lack of cerebral depth and erotic potency. Her *Memoirs* thus form a most incriminating argument against those portrayals of the robust hero so pervasive in the Wellington literature and portraiture, a man whose death would inspire "a masculine, loyal, deep yet elevating sorrow, such as befits the fall of a soldier-prince."[66] The *Memoirs*, however, also implicate Wellington in adultery and sexual intemperance, moral failings that most middle-class Victorians would have found lurid, even offensive. Wilson's Wellington is an absurd, tedious creature but also a lustful and predatory one.

Shortly after "the terrific Duke of Wellington! the wonder of the world!!" is announced by Wilson's housekeeper on his first visit to Wilson's home, he is represented as a nose-blowing, pompous, inarticulate boob, offering one hundred guineas for a rendezvous that Wilson agrees to only with reluctance: "I have heard of his grace often, said I [to the housekeeper], in a tone of deep disappointment. . . . Well, thought I, with a sigh! I suppose he must come."[67] The double entendre of this last observation is played out wittily as Wilson describes subsequent meetings with the duke, whose social dexterity is represented as being no less deficient than his sexual skills.

Wilson does not merely deride Wellington as a lover but also actually lampoons his most celebrated quality, common sense, with its connotations of self-mastery, laconic detachment, and objectivity, as the attribute that makes him an impaired, tongue-tied suitor: "Wellington called on me. . . . I tried him on every subject I could muster. On all, he was most impenetrably taciturn. At last he started an original idea of his own. . . . I wonder you do not get married, Harriette! (By-the-bye, ignorant people are always wondering.) Why so? Wellington, however, gives no reason for anything unconnected with fighting . . . and he, therefore, again became silent."[68] Impenetrability and taciturnity, generally figured as both the rudiments and signs of Wellington's strategic brilliance, are here turned into handicaps.

Maxwell's effort to construct an enduring, morally commendable image of Wellington requires the deliberate exclusion of anecdotal material such as Wilson's. The presence of the *Memoirs* in Maxwell's *Life*, however, is revealed in those vociferous protestations against the merest hint of contradiction, editorial interjections that testify powerfully to the existence of antithetical narrative projects, even if these are not identified with any precision. Scorning Wilson's lively anecdotes as perfidious myth unworthy of attention, Maxwell absolves his subject of any moral stain even as he attempts to shine a more exhaustive and "truer light" on Wellington's character and actions.

But what would be the result of a study that embraced rather than censured the "manifold myth" that follows "after death"? This endeavor would entail a more generous understanding of both myth and after-ness than that offered by Maxwell. It would, in fact, insist on the mythologizing propensities of Maxwell, Hughes, and the anonymous authors of posthumous tributes in the *Times* and the *ILN*. Roland Barthes's definition of myth as "a type of speech chosen by history" supplies a useful alternative to the version Maxwell indicts.[69] Asserting that "everything can be a myth provided it is conveyed by a discourse," Barthes opens the language of mass culture to the activity of deciphering.[70] *Myth* in this sense connotes neither intentional deception nor false consciousness but helps to explain how certain discourses attain symbolic and ideological status in particular social formations at particular moments in time. This understanding of myth inaugurates the interpretive work undertaken in the following chapters.

To return briefly to *Tom Brown's School Days* by way of example: Hughes's novel can be comprehended as operating within myth's "peculiar system, in that it is constructed from a semiological chain which existed before it"[71]—a system that responds to a renewed British interest in the nature of masculinity and the goals of education in 1857. On what Barthes calls the readily evident level of the sign, the novel celebrates robust laddishness, casting Tom as the pedagogically useful model of proto-manhood who gradually becomes "conscious of his new social position and dignities, and . . . luxuriate[s] in the realized ambition of being a public school-boy."[72] On the level of myth, of the "mere signifier" that takes the sign as its "raw material,"[73] Hughes's novel interpolates through brief allusions those popular stories about Wellington—the preexisting semiological chain of heroic myth—that had made him a ubiquitous hero figure during the previous half century.

Whether speaking of a novel that takes Wellington and his exploits as part of its raw material or of a biography that thoroughly exonerates in order to stabilize its subject, we can take as a premise Graham Dawson's claim that "the very possibility of the soldier hero is . . . a narrative construct."[74] Whereas common sense would seem to affirm that heroic storytelling gives straightforward textual embodiment to the real heroic qualities of British soldiers, I would argue along with Dawson that, "on the contrary, the heroism and virtue of the patriotic soldier is secured, not by his actions, but by their narration."[75] A critical investigation of this storytelling might fruitfully turn to the Great Exhibition of 1851, which has, like Wellington, been the subject of manifold myth and which in a number of intriguing ways functioned as a rehearsal for the duke's own funeral.

TWO

First Rehearsal

Exhibition

THE STORY of the Crystal Palace and its assembly of manufactured articles in Hyde Park has been so frequently rehearsed that the 1851 exhibition's status as one of "the most influential representative bod[ies] of the nineteenth century" is now widely accepted,[1] even if its capacity to successfully advertise and champion Britain's industrial supremacy has been seriously questioned in recent years. "The Great Exhibition of the Industry of All Nations" has been portrayed as an event that evoked the Victorian temper in singular ways, even as "the authentic voice of British capitalism in the hour of its greatest triumph."[2] Its preeminence as a landmark event on the Victorian social and economic scene was also well documented by its early sponsors, who went to great lengths to advertise the glassed-in spectacle of goods as an inimitable, international tournament, "one of the most splendid and remarkable undertakings that has ever been attempted in [England] or any other country."[3] With its profitable, 141-day run, six million visitors, and fourteen thousand exhibitors, the exhibition appeared to many to have been an unmitigated success. Its triumvirate of founding fathers (Henry Cole of the Public Records Office, Prince Albert as president of the Royal Commission, and Joseph Paxton as the Crystal Palace's chief architect) was immediately and repeatedly extolled as an enlightened body cultivating Britain's continued ascendancy in a competitive, international marketplace. The year 1851 "really [did] mark the high point when the nation's self-confidence was as yet unshaken," ran the common estimation, "and when no Englishman would have admitted the possibility that other nations might one day equal, let alone surpass, Great Britain."[4] It is now generally recognized that this assessment was highly inadequate as a gloss on the moment of the exhibition, which was as much a response to anxieties about industrial capability as it was an undiluted celebration of Britain's superiority in this domain.[5]

The exhibition, however, also offers a unique, richly allusive point of contact with the Duke of Wellington in the year preceding his death. This is a subplot well worth outlining, in part because the "Great Exhibition of Things"[6] functioned as an immediate precedent, temporally and geographically, for the exhibition of the Great Man's corpse. In the funeral might be located the sedimentations and symptoms of the master narrative composed by the exhibition.

Bell's Life in London was explicit in its comparison of the funeral to the exhibition, foregrounding the more recent ceremony against a now surpassed spectacle, the latter already regarded as fading into history: "Within the metropolis were congregated more persons than were contained in the whole of England 300 years ago—a greater population than all of Scotland has now . . . very far greater than the population of London itself in that year of the Great Exhibition which appeared then the culminating point of the age of great cities."[7] *Bell's* arithmetic is rather specious; the unsubstantiated correlation between superseded populations and the number of spectators briefly congregated to witness the funeral cortege is analogically useless, a comparison of apples with oranges. In terms of actual attendance, the exhibition topped the funeral by a margin of at least four to one.

Still, in its very excess, in its fascination with numbers, and in its attempt to evaluate the historical significance of events through numerical tally and contrast, the newspaper points toward a peculiarly Victorian compulsion to translate into pithy narrative the national appreciation for imposing pageantry. Wellington's actual involvement in the magnificent opening of the Crystal Palace to the first twenty-five thousand ticket holders—which included his procession through the length of the building arm in arm with Waterloo veteran Henry Paget to the royal dais, where the two elderly heroes joined the queen, prince, royal chancellor, and numerous other dignitaries—elicited for those assembled to witness the scene a vivid sense of national and historical realization. Wellington's physical presence at this moment of high festival reminded spectators of their collective debt to those who had destroyed Napoleon's menace thirty-six years earlier and who had (so it was commonly argued) ushered in an extended period of peace and subsequent affluence; the duke's death in the following year would be read as having occurred "at the beginning of the mid-Victorian golden age, the two decades of prosperity, stability and even complacency which followed the self-congratulatory 1851 Crystal Palace Exhibition."[8] Wellington was positioned by one aggrandizing versifier as the framer of

> Commerce boundless—Freedom sure.—
> Based upon divine foundations—
> Our holy Faith unshaken—pure:
> Our flag triumphant, throne secure—
> Our Queen the arbitress of nations.[9]

"Think you," another Wellington commemorator was to ask, "that the crystal palace would ever have been seen, or that you would have witnessed the peaceful and scientific fraternity of the whole world's population in your own little island? Think you, that you would have seen all this if Napoleon had conquered at Waterloo?"[10]

In turn, Prince Albert's perseverance and defiance of all risks of failure warranted his construction in the public mind as the genius singularly responsible for getting the exhibition off the ground and making London the center of the world. Victoria gave sole credit to her husband for the "*touching* spectacle" of the opening on 1 May, "the *greatest* day in our history," rhapsodizing that "Albert's dearest name is immortalised with this *great* conception, *his* own, and my *own* dear country *showed* she was *worthy* of it."[11] Wellington's position on the platform as part of the select group next to Victoria and Albert, however, served as a memento of even greater exertions made on behalf of the nation, exertions that laid the foundation for England to issue its "hospitable invitation to surrounding nations to bring the choicest products of their industry to her capital, and there to enter into an amicable competition with each other and with herself."[12]

The duke's own funeral, then, to which Nicholas Michell claimed "a Nation . . . [came] to drop a tear," had a kind of trial run with that "congress of the world's genius and industry" in which Wellington himself played an ancillary role.[13] If "a world seemed met . . . to honour [Wellington's] great funeral rite," then London could boast of having been a global host on two grand occasions in as many years. During the first of these, the duke also discharged his duties as the recently appointed ranger of Hyde Park, a sinecure position that the rheumatic octogenarian took very seriously. Responsible for "clearing" the once-royal park and maintaining order within its boundaries during the construction of the Crystal Palace, Wellington's position as ranger marked the final, official stage in his protracted career as an effective manager of the public order. In a gesture that foreshadowed anxieties about crowd control for his own funeral, a subject I touch upon in chapter 4, Wellington suggested that at least fifteen thousand police officers be hired to keep the area around Hyde Park safe for the exhibition after 26 May, once the Crystal Palace was opened to the masses on "Shilling Days."

This role had been practiced with great acclaim three years earlier, when Wellington arranged the defense of London against Chartists who had gathered on Kennington Common, intending to march on Westminster to present their third national petition. At that time, according to Jeffrey Auerbach, "although the government, remembering the Peterloo massacre of 1819 and the negative consequences of creating martyrs, exercised great restraint in dealing with the Chartist gathering . . . the mob in April 1848—estimated at around 25,000—produced virtual middle-class hysteria."[14] Wellington's skillful disposition of constables and troops on that threatening day of 10 April was his last act of military planning. Praise was ubiquitous among antiradical publications for the "military preparations, almost unparalleled for extent and completeness, made by the illustrious Duke at the head of the army to put down any insurrectionary attempts that might be made."[15] These preparations also ensured that Wellington's name would be forever associated with the ultimate "failure" of a working-class movement that had for ten years threatened social revolution but that lost much of its impetus when the petitioners quietly dispersed on the south side of the Thames. (This association had one very literal aspect. The parliamentary committee that examined the petition reported large numbers of forgeries among the approximately two million signatures: Wellington's signature was included seventeen times.) Symbolically, there could be no more trenchant representation of class antagonism in the late 1840s than this confrontation between a constabulary organized by a notoriously aristocratic peer, "a pedigree gentleman . . . [who] combined with a high sense of duty the narrowness that comes from inherited convictions,"[16] and the massed forces of working men led by Feargus O'Connor. And there could be no more triumphant pronouncement of the promise held for economic and social prosperity in the postrevolutionary, post-Chartist 1850s than the appearance of the duke at the exhibition, still relatively fresh from having put a final stop to the potential "irruption of a dangerous rabble."[17]

The defense of London, however, differed considerably from the more mundane task of managing Hyde Park, the most dramatic event of which involved the expulsion from its precincts of a certain Mrs. Hicks, a well-established squatter who sold cakes and springwater from her tiny cottage near the Serpentine and to whose defense the North London Antienclosure Society came with some indignation. Having "taken up the case of Mrs. Hicks with a view of attaining for her . . . redress," the organization's secretary wrote to Wellington, asking if "that ill-used individual, without even offer of compensation for the loss she sustained, and the injury suffered," would be afforded justice, "as we consider that at least she is entitled to the value of her building so destroyed."[18] Wellington declined to correspond with the representative of a private society. In a sense, he was not only fulfilling to the letter of the law his duties as ranger but also protecting property—a sacred trust to the old Tory—upon which he could stake a personal claim. His opinion of Paxton's design for the exhibition building had been solicited by Prince Albert, and the duke's affirmation that "it would do" lent both credibility and respectability to a project over which he became a sort of high priest, his frequent visits to the exhibition never failing to arouse great excitement among the spectators.

These anecdotes about Wellington's various associations with the exhibition, in which a man primarily identified with the arts of war was effortlessly requisitioned to play an honorific part in a "Diorama of the Peaceful Arts,"[19] illustrate two closely related aspects about the nature of Victorian spectacles and the ways in which prominent individuals could contribute to their success. First, the exhibition demonstrated that Wellington had been thoroughly deified as England's Grand Old Man, tempered by earlier political strife and conditioned to serve the imperatives of national pageantry. Second, Wellington's performance at the exhibition was based on a sophisticated script that had the primary goal of foregrounding national superiority.

Regarding the first of these, Wellington's incipient position within the pantheon of British war heroes was being gradually solidified throughout the 1840s, but only in heated rivalry with antagonists who contested his reputation as an intrepid leader. In the first half of the 1840s, various of the duke's more contentious acts as prime minister (from 1828 to 1830 and in 1834) and as a member of the Tory Opposition were still vivid in the collective memory: his introduction in 1829 of the Catholic Relief Bill despite objections from a large minority within his own party (and his subsequent duel with the Earl of Winchilsea over accusations of betrayal); his stubborn opposition to parliamentary reform, most notoriously articulated in his 1830 House of Lords speech against Earl Grey's and Earl Russell's amendments to the franchise; his reluctance to oppose the Test and Corporation Acts; and his nonintervention in the East after the Battle of Navarino. Wellington's antireform stance, in particular, earned him widespread infamy, which resulted most notoriously in a mob attack on Apsley House during which bricks were lobbed through the mansion's windows.

Wellington was, therefore, in need of public reclamation. For some years after the first Reform Bill of 1832, he was remembered as its most vociferous opponent and, to quote Maxwell's theatrical prose, was "lowered to the depth of odium. Coarse reproach and bloodthirsty menace were yelled at him from the very throats which, only a few years before, had ached with unceasing cheers."[20] Harriet Arbuthnot, wife to Charles, joint secretary of the treasury during the duke's first ministry, succinctly outlined Wellington's fears about parliamentary reform in a journal entry for 29 March 1831: "[Wellington] thinks, if [the bill] carried, that a revolution is inevitable, that a reformed House of Commons will immediately attack the tithes and the West Indies, that all property will become insecure, that the funds will fall, the revenues not be paid and that, when once we get into financial difficulties, our whole frame will be dislocated and destroyed!"[21] An unwavering Wellington worshiper and High Tory, Arbuthnot believed that "England is gone perfectly mad . . . in their desire to have this nonsensical Bill."[22] The duke's intense paranoia about levelers and critics of imperialist policy, however, forced the otherwise acclamatory *Illustrated London News* to admit that he was "an obstinate and bigoted worshiper of the past in legislation,"[23] and popular opprobrium directed at him led one biographer to lament "the way of the British," who "always tire of their heroes of yesterday."[24]

Equally as damning, perhaps, was Benjamin Disraeli's censure in the third chapter of his best-known and most politically motivated novel, *Sybil*, first published in 1845. Introducing his narrative with a brief historical sketch of British parliamentary turmoil in the early nineteenth century, Disraeli eventually referred to the collapse of Wellington's ministry in 1830 and was led to ask, "How comes it . . . that so great a man, in so great a position, wrecked his party, and so completely annihilated his political position, that, even with his historical reputation to sustain him, he can since only re-appear in the councils of his sovereign in a subordinate, not to say equivocal, character?"[25] Although the early sections of *Sybil* must be read in part as a template for a new kind of Toryism, a jockeying for position on the part of the author and member of Parliament to distinguish his own political ambitions from a bankrupt conservative tradition, few would have disagreed that Wellington was a far better soldier than politician.

By the time of the exhibition, however, "the Duke's frequent visits to the [Crystal Palace] as it went up were invariably met with cheers from the workmen and visitors, equally invariably acknowledged with one finger raised to the hat brim and no change of countenance. The hisses, boos and brickbats of 1831, when he opposed the Reform Bill, were forgotten."[26] As a trial run for the duke's own funeral, the exhibition proved that his once-tarnished reputation as a blundering politician and, for a time, the most hated man in England had been completely made over; through its adoration, the public of 1851 displayed a willingness to canonize Wellington by making him an integral component of a "great peace-offering to mankind."[27] The narrative rehabilitation of a man who in 1830 had "quitted office in the dusk of discredit and under the chill disapproval of all parties"[28] but who by the early 1850s once again "commanded the very highest universal respect and reverence"[29] was tested by Wellington's habitual presence in the Crystal Palace during the four months it remained open. Whereas many of the other products exhibited were disparaged as useless gadgets ("we may look at a tissue which nobody could wear; at a carriage in which nobody could ride; at a fireplace which no servant could clean if it were ever guilty of a fire"[30]), Wellington was not found wanting. In the context of the Crystal Palace, that monument to production, the duke was a vestige of a more austere and chivalrous age whose values were much cherished despite their apparent supersession by a new and pervasive culture of commodities. Home Secretary Lord Palmerston could write to his younger brother, Sir William Temple, that with the loss of "our great Duke," England had also lost a political icon whose "name was a tower of strength abroad, and his opinions and counsel . . . valuable at home. No man ever lived or died in the possession of more unanimous love respect and esteem from his Countrymen."[31]

Here, we touch upon the second aspect mentioned earlier, the dramatic scripting of the exhibition with Wellington playing a central role. The procession through the Crystal Palace's main nave recalled to historically conscious viewers (as would the duke's funeral procession some eighteen months later) the great pageants and entries of sixteenth-century Europe or, indeed, the annual tours instituted by the Duchess of Kent's comptroller in 1832 to formally present Princess Victoria to the nation— excursions King William referred to sarcastically as "Royal Progresses." The peregrinations of Elizabeth I or Charles V, ordered according to a rigorous social hierarchy and designed to inspire towns and cities under monarchical dominion with renewed loyalty through spectacular display, found new applications in increasingly democratic, nineteenth-century Britain. In the case of the child Victoria, the progress was revived chiefly as a means of introducing the country to the future queen while also familiarizing her with its geography and people. In turn, the exhibition procession drew upon the progress in its formal arrangement and introduced to foreign visitors a royal couple largely reduced to symbolic status. As one scholar has put it, "The monarchy's success arose from its transformation into a popular spectacle during the nineteenth century; it was during that time that the association between royal spectacle and middle-class practices and values came to seem the permanent hallmark of the royal family."[32] Victoria and Albert's presence, however, was essential to the effective advertising of the United Kingdom's industrial superiority. Behind the royals and great officers of the household, followed by a chorus of cheers, came the "Commander-in-Chief and the Master of the Ordnance (Wellington and Anglesey), arm-in-arm to support each other's hobbling (the Duke from rheumatism and the Marquess on the artificial leg which replaced the one blown off at Waterloo) and talking away in the penetrating tones of the very deaf loudly enough to be heard above the bellowing of Willis's great organ."[33] The procession staged English history from the Napoleonic past to the commodity-rich present. The participating Waterloo veterans were prime artifacts from a time when Britain was at war with France, once "that Empire Unright, / The spawn of anarchy and godless years, / Hatched in the refuse of an ebbing faith,"[34] now transformed through a friendly rivalry that benefited from "the noble spirit of emulation, devoid of its former rancorous prejudices, which [the exhibition] . . . generated between [England and France]."[35]

Considered side by side, the two aspects just described hint at a cultural subtext laced with its own tensions and contradictions that the technological apotheosis of the exhibition—and Wellington's central place in it—sought to resolve. Anthony Bird touches upon the complex dynamics of this attempted resolution in his verdict that the duke "reached the end of his life as the Victorian age, exemplified in the Crystal Palace, reached its apogee."[36] Interpreted retrospectively in this way, Wellington's soon-to-be death converged apocryphally with another culmination. As if there was an immanent connection, the expiry of the aged hero was allied with the perfection—and hence, inevitable subsequent decline—of Britain's industrial prowess, which, in turn, "exemplified . . . the Victorian age." Both of these endings, however, were inscribed within the rhetoric of renewal. In the exhibition and funeral, then, spectators encountered some form of self-denouement, despite the ubiquitous, popular language of revival. With both events, the Victorians were confronted with the triumphal melancholy of decay.

On the one hand, the duke's funeral was an occasion for mourners to "catch a new spark of patriotism and new incitements to heroic self-denial in the service of their cherished country,"[37] just as the exhibition was to prove British industrial supremacy. On the other, there could be no denying that the last great hero of the Napoleonic era was gone forever ("Death speaks to dust the mighty one, / And conquers conquering Wellington"[38]), just as the exhibition itself was conceived in part through the anxious recognition that by the mid-1840s, British technical superiority was being increasingly challenged by French and German design and decoration. "Even as early as 1851," David Newsome observes,

> British engineers had noted at the Great Exhibition three inventions capable in time of mass-production, all of them products of American engineering: the sewing-machine, the Colt revolver and the mechanical reaper. . . . The most serious threat to British industry and commerce, however, was posed by the phenomenal progress in industrialization on the Continent, notably in Germany, Belgium and France. . . . What was happening . . . was that other countries were catching up at a rate of acceleration that meant they would soon exceed the productivity of the once acknowledged "workshop of the world."[39]

So, if Wellington's funeral cannot be adequately comprehended as simply the pinnacle of "the palmy days of the great funeral,"[40] the exhibition should not be read uncritically through the words of its tireless promoter, Henry Cole, who spoke approvingly of "a great people invit[ing] all civilized nations to a festival, to bring into comparison the works of human skill."[41] In fact, Britain came to terms with its own waning industrial dominance by representing what was essentially an unbalanced arena for the prominent and overwhelming display of British goods—half of the Crystal Palace's floor space was reserved for the products of Britain and its colonies—as a "noble and disinterested plan," an equitable "arena for the exhibition of the industrial triumphs of the whole world."[42] The ultimate "impartial verdict" on the exhibition was declared in the *Illustrated Catalogue:* "It is to the honour of Great Britain that, notwithstanding the generous risk incurred by inviting competitors from all the nations of the world—prepared as they had been by long years of successful study and practical experience—the fame of *British* manufacturers has been augmented by this contest."[43] Accounts of a neutral "comparison" of products therefore obscured the competitive and sometimes bitter struggle for survival in and domination of the global market of commodities, a struggle in which the floor plan of the Crystal Palace gave Britain a critical advantage.

Therefore, 1851 stood as a year of jubilee for British capitalism and the exhibition as an event that "display[ed] the preeminence of Britain's own industry over the rest of the world."[44] The latter, however, must also be grasped as an imaginary resolution of material contradictions. Those contradictions were signaled by the seeming incompatibility between England's extension of a nonpartisan, "hospitable invitation" to surrounding nations and the assertion that, "when his Royal Highness Prince Albert issues his summons to another competition, British supremacy will be manifested in every branch of Industrial Art."[45] The imaginary resolution to these contradictions resided in the inequalities of the Crystal Palace's spatial division, which guaranteed that, "although the exhibition originated from internationalist sentiments, it could and would be presented and interpreted in nationalistic terms."[46]

Here, the venerable Wellington once again came in. His formal affiliation with the great contest between "civilized" nations would have lent a rather different meaning to the much vaunted phrase *amicable competition*, especially for French exhibitors who may have interpreted his presence as a subdued reminder of the more inclement competition between Europe's chief imperial powers earlier in the century. (According to members of the Royal Commission, half of the sixty thousand foreign visitors to the exhibition were French.) More interesting, however, was Wellington's appointment as a subject in a symbolic act of triple veneration. Franz Xaver

Winterhalter's *The First of May* immortalizes this secular adoration with true éclat (figure 2.1). In this painting, the German artist, who was already enjoying a successful career with his portraits of European royalty, falls back upon a cherished story about Wellington's fidelity to the Crown to accomplish his immortalization of the social and political elect. One of the roles reserved for Wellington in his later years and commonly expressed in sentimental accolades was that of the "veritable guide, philosopher, and friend of the Royal Family"—"it was to him that the Queen and Prince Albert instinctively turned in any difficulty."[47] *The First of May* celebrates this privileged relationship while also alluding to its own distinctive historical moment.

Painted to commemorate the shared birthdays of Wellington and his godson, Prince Arthur, on 1 May and the opening of the exhibition by the queen on the same date in 1851, Winterhalter's canvas presents viewers with an unsurprising nineteenth-century trinity: royals, the duke, and, silhouetted against the setting sun in the left background, the Crystal Palace —a pictorial idealization that unites the past (Wellington as patriarchal magus), present (the royal couple, emblem of the nation's welfare), and future (the infant prince but also the palace, with its revolutionary design that seemed to put it "ahead of its time"[48]). The painting therefore constitutes a fanciful totality in which temporal discontinuity, attenuated royal prerogative, and the precariousness of industrial superiority are positively mediated. It is more accurate, however, to speak of the painting's function as a reconstitution of a totality that was always already jeopardized: by midcentury, Britain, the cradle of the Industrial Revolution and once extolled as the workshop to the world, suffered diminishing repute as a leader in design and production, an eclipse that could only be suspended through the imagistic appropriation of nationally recognized figures such as Wellington and the royals.

In *The First of May,* the elder Arthur plays foil to his namesake in an act of mutual exchange. In the twilight of life and the half-light of the canvas, Wellington offers to the infant—in the symbolic form of the miniature casket—the legacy of an august career, now the child's and his generation's salubrious inheritance. In turn, proffering a cluster of lilies of the valley, the illuminated child-prince figures as the personification of spring,

FIGURE 2.1 *The First of May, 1851*, by Franz Xaver Winterhalter. The Royal Collection © 2002, Her Majesty Queen Elizabeth II.

a promise of newness that refracts upon the other figures and artifacts in the painting, which declare, in toto, "England shall be great (again)!"

This was the same message tendered by Wellington's funeral and cultivated by a profuse exhibition of fetishized (and fetishizing) Wellingtonian merchandise, reminiscent of the goods displayed at the Crystal Palace. If the exhibition was depicted as Albert's most resplendent achievement, commemoration of the duke's death on 14 September 1852 was to be remembered as a similar, "national" occasion, inspired by Victoria's request that the army mourn for Wellington as it would for the death of a member of the royal family and by her insistence that the funeral be postponed until Parliament reconvened in November so that it could lend official approval to the obsequies. The announcement was therefore sent out that her Majesty . . . [is] anxious that the greatest possible number of her subjects should have an opportunity of joining it [the tribute], is anxious, above all, that such honours should not appear to emanate from the Crown alone, and that the two Houses of Parliament should have an opportunity . . . of stamping the proposed ceremony with increased solemnity. . . . The body of the Duke of Wellington will, therefore, remain, with the concurrence of his family, under proper guardianship, until the Queen shall have received the formal approval of Parliament of the course which it will be the duty of her Majesty's servants to submit to both houses upon their reassembling.[49]

Like the exhibition, which encouraged the attendance of the working classes by admitting people at one-fifth the usual price on Shilling Days, the funeral was to be apprehended as a fundamentally democratic affair, an undertaking of "the people."[50] Although a project specifically conceived by the queen, it was to be by and for her "subjects," aptly represented by the Commons and Lords and repeatedly subsumed under the more comprehensive designation of "the English nation."

"The Exhibition proved once and for all," Thomas Richards has argued, "that the best way to sell things to the English was to sell them the culture and ideology of England, its plans for commercial dominance, its dreams of Empire, its social standards, and its codes of conduct."[51] Likewise, the funeral confirmed that the hero's corpse could be recast as a commanding icon that had a double referent combining a mythology of monumental English tradition and racial uniformity (wherein Englishness and "the people" were amalgamated into the powerful talisman of "the English people") with an ideal of heroic hypermasculinity. A result of the stabilization of Wellington's reified image was therefore those now-conventional biographical allusions to a man whose "life-long determination [was] to act rightly if possible, 'manfully' in any case" and who embodied the "chief virtues" of the English at their best, "truthfulness, courage, honesty, fairness . . . directness, forwardness, decision and realism."[52] The next chapter is dedicated to an exploration of this double function.

THREE

Second Rehearsal

Simplicity

B EARING in mind that both exhibition and funeral were caught up in the same enterprise—the enhancement of national prestige via the pomp and circumstance of public display, as well as the marketing of English goods and of Englishness itself—the actual staging of the funeral can be viewed as an impressive exercise in deft planning and organization. Wellington's death came quickly, and even two months' time for funeral preparations was barely sufficient. The death, however, could not properly be called unexpected. His advanced age, combined with an extended history of "epileptic fits" that began as early as 1839,[1] caused Wellington's nephew, Edward, stationed in South Africa, to write stoically to his brother about an apparent rumor in the press that was eventually corroborated: "I received a number of newspapers . . . by the last mail. A report which I do not believe also arrived that the Duke had died, sent by telegraph as the steamer was leaving England, as there have been reports of this sort before I trust this one is not true, although as he has now reached Lord Wellesley's age and has gone through more hardships in his early life we cannot hope he can live much longer."[2]

Three years earlier, Wellington himself had expressed aggravation about persistent reports of his own death. "I observed the paragraph in the papers about my being sick," he wrote to Angela Burdett-Coutts, a regular correspondent; "it was reported in London and on the Road that I was Dead.... The fact is that I have had nothing the matter with me.... I am always annoyed by these Reports."[3] But if the public and his own relatives were prepared for news of Wellington's death, the actual event was immediately and repeatedly represented as a shock to the social and political fabric of the national and indeed the international community. "I ... do most truly lament," wrote William Spicer, in a letter that echoed the sentiments of the press, "the great affliction which all nations have sustained by the sudden demise of the greatest man in the universe. The scene at Walmer must be heartrending."[4]

Wellington's death, which came after a series of strokes in the quiet and seclusion of Walmer Castle on the Essex coast, signaled a personal ending that contrasted noticeably with the "eccentric romanticism" and "strange wildness" that were to mark the public's solemnization of the hero's passing in the coming months.[5] Simplicity, in fact, became a code word for Wellington's demise. John Wilson thought it worthwhile to note in his copious biography that "the Duke's bed-room, in each of his residences, was little better than a barrack bivouac. His bed, even to his last night, was more narrow and simple than that of a subaltern."[6] A line engraving of Wellington's bedroom at Apsley House, copied from a drawing made shortly before the duke's death, registers the acclaimed austerity of both the typical ducal chamber and its occupant (figure 3.1). Images such as this, in which the modestly dressed yet graceful old man is silhouetted by window light that also illuminates the room's bare walls and unencumbered carpet, testify compellingly to Wellingtonian simplicity.

The national press, in turn, was fascinated with the death room at Walmer. The fact that the duke "occupied only *one room*,"[7] which served simultaneously as library, study, and bedroom, confirmed his popular renown as a man of exceptional, if also characteristically English, frugality and proved that he died in a way that "was in accordance with his character— simple ... and unostentatious."[8] The *Illustrated London News* published a unique view of the room, a death scene for which the artist, Joseph

FIGURE 3.1 *The Duke of Wellington's Bed Room*, by T. H. Ellis, after F. Shephard, 1853. © National Portrait Gallery, London.

Williams, "selected" certain persons in order to create a "historical picture" that would reinforce and perhaps secure for posterity Wellington's reputation for dignified composure (figure 3.2). The illustration contains a number of anomalies. Neither Lord nor Lady Wellesley was actually present at the death, but the caption indicates that Wellington is still alive, experiencing his "last moments" as his son and daughter-in-law lean, engrossed, on his chair. Wellington also suffered no fewer than four "fits" in the hours before his death, the first of "a rather violent character" and each subsequent convulsion "of a greater violence and . . . still more severe than the preceding ones."[9] Yet he is portrayed in a placid, sleeplike attitude, the unconscious but evidently serene focus of medical and familial scrutiny.[10] Although committed to presenting an accurate depiction of this moving spectacle in order to fulfill a contract the paper had made with readers to provide "every interesting feature and characteristic" of Wellington's life and death,[11] the *ILN* also accommodates itself to the formal requirements of the tableau in this illustration. In the absence of definitive information about what actually took place in the chamber at Walmer, the *ILN* appeals to the drama of the situation by "freezing" the group of intent observers, producing the picturesque effect typical of the tableau. Creating a striking situation through the participants' act of holding position around the duke's body, the object of meaning, the illustration also invites viewers to attribute special symbolic import to this moment of seemingly private grief: Wellington's death is a national tragedy. The rapt eyewitnesses appear to understand the significance of the event and assume the solemnly attentive attitudes befitting their roles as players in history.

One London clergyman exhorted his congregation to take to heart a picture very similar to this one as an edifying instance of Wellington's self-denial: "I exceedingly admire, and would strongly recommend . . . the picture of the little chamber in Walmer Castle, in which [Wellington] died —his study, library, and bedroom; the most instructive, if not the most interesting, of the vast series of pictures concerning him."[12] Wellington's unceremonious death, then, was particularly appropriate for a much honored hero who nevertheless spurned the plush comforts of feathered mattresses and pillows in favor of the military cot on which he was rumored to sleep every night after quitting the fields of Waterloo. More significantly, the death represented yet another instance fit for emulation; in it, good Anglicans could "admire [Wellington's] clearness of discernment, correctness of judgement, rectitude in public business; and emulate the example."[13]

This emphasis on Wellington's notorious austerity and the simplicity of his death forms an important footnote in the story of what was about to become an opulent postmortem celebration, "one of the most magnificent and solemn pageants recorded in history . . . such as the world, no doubt, has never seen since the triumphal marches of Rome's imperial conquerors."[14] Homespun simplicity and common sense, after all, were the traits most widely cherished by and attributed to the English themselves. "We need cultivate no warlike tastes," Charles Boutell counseled his parishioners at Litcham, "in order to emulate the example of Wellington. Law and Order, Loyalty and Patriotism, Self-denial and Self-devotion, —let us follow him in these."[15] Since Wellington was proclaimed by the nation's voice to be a model Englishman, an embodied expression of the essential attributes of the people, English mourners could do no better

FIGURE 3.2 *Last Moments of the Duke of Wellington, Illustrated London News,*
13 November 1852.

than pattern their own behavior after a man whose governing principles
were supposed to be order, loyalty, a sense of duty, a devotion to right authority, and an abnegation of self. "Children of England," Marie Maurice
exhorted in a brilliant example of how Carlyle's philosophy of hero worship could be turned to practical application in any situation, "great and
noble as Wellington was, here are qualities you can all imitate. This is the

stuff out of which heroes are made, whether they have to fight on battle-fields, or to wage a quieter war within."[16] W. R. H. Trowbridge provided what is perhaps the most succinct expression of this transference: "England followed the example [Wellington] had set her and did her duty by him. . . . She covered herself with his name, as if it were a mantle."[17]

The metonymic connection here is quite explicit: by honoring Wellington's common sense and attributing to the English a natural predilection for similar opacity, commemorators turned their applause for the duke into an ovation for Englishness. "'Common Sense,'" wrote William Fraser in *Words on Wellington,* a self-consciously pedantic, rambling series of anecdotes published in 1889, "means the collective Wisdom of generations; which is occasionally found concentrated in the mind of one individual, as it was in [the duke's]."[18] "We should think ourselves ungrateful to God, unfaithful to our duty, and unworthy of the name of Englishmen," Richard Glover pontificated, "if we allowed such a great event as the death of Wellington, to pass by without endeavoring to turn it to some profit and advantage."[19] Proper emulation was therefore a matter of good moral economy, most effective when both orator and listener, biographer and reader understood the immediate value of exemplary citation. Maurice cautioned her young readers that they had wasted their time in reading her biography if they did "not rise up from it with [the] determination . . . [to] be more resolute in the performance of every duty, and more earnest in fulfilling, with zeal and diligence, the work given to them."[20] Coming from the pen of the nation's recently laureled poet, Alfred, Lord Tennyson's *Ode on the Death of the Duke of Wellington* offered one of the most widely read eulogies binding together in Wellington the twin ideals of lucidity and discretion:

> Mourn for the man of amplest influence,
> Yet clearest of ambitious crime,
> Our greatest yet with least pretense,
> Great in council and great in war,
> Foremost captain of his time,
> Rich in saving common-sense,
> And, as the greatest only are,
> In his simplicity sublime.[21]

In linking, once again, the hero's simplicity with a native common sense, Tennyson did much to guarantee that these two attributes would continue to define Wellington's personal legacy up until the present day.

Wellington had also been relentlessly positioned as the dutiful hero, a man whose celebrated deference to king or queen helped to buttress the constitutional monarchy and to distinguish him absolutely from revolutionary self-promoters such as Napoleon. In Wellington, Englishness and duty coalesce in unprecedented ways. Again, Tennyson's *Ode* was integral to the popularization of Wellingtonian duty and was explicit about the connection between personal accountability and national obligations. The poet encouraged readers to follow the example of Wellington in their allegiance to that exacting but rewarding mistress, duty:

> Not once or twice in our fair island-story,
> The path of duty was the way to glory:
> He, that ever following her commands,
> On with toil of heart and knees and hands,
> Thro' the long gorge to the far light has won
> His path upward, and prevail'd,
> Shall find the toppling crags of Duty scaled
> Are close upon the shining table-lands
> To which our God Himself is moon and sun.[22]

This passage of the *Ode* bordered on apostrophe, a mode of poetic address that enabled the spontaneous association of Wellington's life story with the national epic, "our fair island-story." The abstract concept of duty was saluted as an attribute peculiar not only to Wellington but also to the nation of which he was the type: the hero would lead the nation along the "path of duty" as both responded to God's ordinance, to "toil [with] heart and knees and hands . . . to the far light."

It is worth considering just a few of the other tributes published immediately after the duke's death in order to better comprehend this typological narrative, wherein duty was confirmed as *the* excellence ensuring Britain's future eminence. The trait that most recommended Wellington "to the highest estimate of humanity," maintained London's *Morning Chronicle*, was "his unwavering recognition of duty."[23] Wellington's "was peculiarly an *English* life," declared the *Morning Herald*, the *Chronicle*'s chief rival, "the life of an English soldier and statesman. . . . *Duty* was the guiding start of his career. His ambition was to serve, not himself, but his country and his Sovereign."[24] The latter tribute to Wellingtonian duty, in fact, anticipated Benedict Anderson's celebrated observation about newspaper reading—that "extraordinary mass ceremony [of] . . . almost precisely simultaneous consumption"—by attributing to writers for the Victorian press a similar consensus of activity. "What more vivid figure for the secular, historically clocked, imagined community can be envisioned,"[25] Anderson asks, than the following account of seemingly incidental unanimity?

> There cannot . . . be a clearer or stronger testimony to any fact than is now before us, when we observe half-a-dozen writers, of widely differing notions, sitting down in different parts of London, on the same evening, to write, on the spur of the moment, on one great topic, and find that, be they what they may—Whig, Tory, Radical, or Peelite— they all agree in one testimony, couched even in the same words— that the governing principle of the Duke of Wellington's life, through a glorious career of sixty years, was simply and solely a sense of duty.[26]

According to the *Examiner*, "The idea of the Duke of Wellington's life was duty. . . . He held himself the servant of the English crown, and had no thought or aim that were not centred there."[27] "*Duty—duty—duty* was incessantly in the lips and thoughts of our illustrious countryman," chimed the *Leeds Mercury*.[28]

Such examples could be proliferated ad nauseam. It is useful to recollect that, in its earliest usage, the word *duty* signified the feudal ideal of the homage due to a superior, usually the lord of a manor. In this sense, it signified submission, deference, and appropriate conduct on the part of one who acknowledged the distinction and political authority of another: one's allegiance to duty contributed to social stability through the accession of sovereignty rather than the pursuit of individual ambition. By insisting that Wellington's true greatness resided in his fealty to Crown and state, commemorators invested in him a kind of heroic self-abnegation that enabled them to identify him directly with the soundness and durability of the nation itself. Whereas Napoleon manipulated state and military apparatuses to buttress his own sublime career, Wellington subordinated self-interest and, in the process, became the prototypically English hero.

More subtly, Wellingtonian Englishness in these various eulogies must be understood as operating tacitly within a framework of broader anti-French sentiment that positioned both Wellington and his compatriots as "true specimens of the English character . . . simply and conscientiously doing our duty,"[29] in opposition to the conniving ambitions of Napoleonic Frenchness and its "adherence to the errors and blasphemies of Rome."[30] Samuel Smiles popularized such distinctions by speaking of Wellington as a "self-denying, conscientious, and truly patriotic" hero in contrast to Napoleon, whose only "aim was 'Glory.'"[31] Ultimately, Wellington's "simple" death complemented both a career that exemplified "wonderful intuition and strong native sense" and a nation imprinted with those same qualities.[32]

It would be inaccurate, however, to suggest that Wellington's reputation as an eminently sensible man, "singled out [in the public imagination] for his logistical skills, his caution and his humanity,"[33] was simply and exclusively a projection of national aspirations via the pens of biographers and journalists. The duke himself embraced the role created for him; increasingly presented as a model of English understatement and doggedness, he developed this impression of himself, allowing the persona to displace the man in a gesture that gratified both the public and himself. A letter Wellington wrote to Harriet Arbuthnot after a meeting with King William IV in 1830 demonstrated how the popular mythology was endorsed by the private subject: "I was received with a sort of cold, irritated contempt and indignation. However, there never was such a triumph of truth and Common Sense over falsehood and Madness. In a short time I convinced him by facts and dates that he had no ground whatever to complain of his Ministers. . . . I am however perfectly satisfied with my Day's Work. It is the genuine triumph of Truth and common Sense brought out in plain Terms."[34] Wellington willingly accommodated himself to broader desires, engaging in a form of mutual exchange with his admirers that allowed both parties to unquestioningly perceive the duke as the exemplary representative of truth and common sense—of empirical facts.

By the time of his death, then, Wellington's simplicity—the estimable if occasionally severe lucidity of the best type of Englishman—was widely regarded to be his defining attribute. Common sense and rectitude, however, were traits developed through adversity; the posthumous biographical literature repeatedly emphasized that Wellingtonian simplicity was constantly assaulted by personal afflictions and abstruse demands from uncomprehending superiors. Tormented and proscribed by bureaucracies and dullards, Wellington achieved greatness by persevering without doubt or remorse.

Wellington's travails, therefore, were typically represented as issuing from two distinct sources, the private/familial and the public/governmental. With regard to the former, one of the most popular anecdotes about the hero's early life had to do with his mother, an uncompromising and unsympathetic woman who was known to favor her seemingly more talented older son, Richard. The boy Arthur's first encumbrance, then, was his domineering mother's depreciation: "This fourth child of six was not highly regarded by his strong-willed mother. . . . The young Arthur was accounted plain if not ugly, devoid of intellectual gifts."[35] As a result of his "relative inferiority," Arthur "was the subject of some concern to his vigilant mother";[36] "'I vow to God, I don't know what I shall do with my awkward son Arthur,' complained Lady Mornington to her daughter-in-law, William's wife. He was 'food for powder and nothing more.'"[37]

Much later, Wellington was to be commiserated with for falling into a disastrous and unequal marriage. By most accounts, Catherine Packenham was a tactless and profoundly unsympathetic mate, unable to discuss the things in which Wellington was interested. What could the great Wellington possibly have in common with the "timid little country mouse, good, worthy, sweet and quite useless to him"?[38] In her unique, book-length examination of the duke's marriage, Joan Wilson concludes that, in their short years together, "[Wellington] had found [Catherine] a weak, argumentative creature, making demands on his valuable time, lacking intelligence, careless in paying household bills, and not above damaging his reputation by fearing to reveal debts to tradesmen incurred by misappropriating the housekeeping money to help a relative."[39]

Harriet Arbuthnot's personal journal provides the most direct evidence for such unflattering commentaries. Referring to one of Wellington's rare outbursts about matters unconnected with government, Arbuthnot summarizes a conversation she held with the duke about Catherine's vari-

ous inadequacies: "He complained heavily to me of his domestic annoy-
ances. The parties at his house are certainly spoilt by the Duchess, for she
is the most abominably silly, stupid woman that ever was born. . . . He never
speaks to her and carefully avoids ever going near her."[40] But Wellington
not only endured his uncomfortable situation, he prevailed. Maxwell notes
with some satisfaction that "in marrying Catherine . . . the cost was a heavy
one, but it was paid without hesitation as a just debt. . . . Unlike many men
who have played great parts in the world's history, Wellington never sub-
mitted his will to a woman's; although very susceptible of the influence of
beauty and wit, he treated women either as agreeable companions or as
playthings. He never allowed them to control his actions."[41] Wellington's
capacity to objectify and even discount women as nuisances is a sign of
the latter's single-minded pursuit of higher and infinitely more important
duties. Control, a prerequisite of useful action, requires the radical exclusion of disorienting female influence.

Compounding his afflictions at home, Wellington as a commander
on the field had to contend endlessly against a suspicious public, bungling
fellow officers, inconsistent government bureaucrats, and bellicose members of the Opposition. As one anonymous historian concludes, however,
these "difficulties of the most arduous kind," like the war against France,
were ultimately "terminated, with unexampled glory to England and its
army— . . . a struggle commenced with ambiguous views and prosecuted
with doubtful expectations, but carried to a triumphant conclusion by the
extraordinary genius of a single man."[42] Other biographers point out that
Wellington, like Britain itself during the period of Napoleonic conflict,
was invariably shortchanged of everything that he needed to successfully
complete his job on the field. According to Elizabeth Longford, the duke's
"real concern . . . [throughout his military career was] with the Opposition's scathing abuse. They had never wholeheartedly backed this . . .
Peninsular expedition, nor the choice of commander."[43] "It was not in the
nature of things," Maxwell concludes, "that one in such a peculiarly influential position as the Duke of Wellington should avoid incurring the hostility of parties and persons."[44]

The point of these various records of adversity, all of which locate
sources of the most deleterious resistance in the very individuals who
should have devoted their energies to helping Wellington, is that the hero

always triumphs. His military achievements are all the more remarkable because they had to be forged on a double front. First, Wellington frequently had to contend with superior enemy forces. Individual battles are often recounted in the "forlorn hope" mode, emphasizing the extreme disadvantages faced by the hero in terms of numbers and resources. Maxwell represents the Battle of Assaye in 1803 as an unlikely victory for the British, a profoundly meaningful turning point during which Major-General Wellesley "had to decide between an immediate and offensive movement with 7,500 men and 17 guns against an enemy numbering 50,000 with 128 guns, strongly posted, and a retreat. . . . It was one of those moments in which the renown of an individual is made or marred—the destiny of an empire shattered or confirmed."[45] The *Morning Herald* abridges Wellesley's experiences in India as a perennial struggle against imposed deficiencies: "The scanty means at his disposal, and the enormous masses against which he was obliged to operate, could only be equalised by the most scientific combinations, the most judicious dispositions, and the most rapid evolutions: in all of these he evinced the most decided military genius."[46]

Second, the duke was frustrated by the more mundane and ultimately more fatiguing machinations of the home government. When, along with fellow generals Hew Dalrymple and Harry Burrard, Wellesley was recalled to London in November 1808 to face a court of inquiry accusing British officers of allowing French commander Andoche Junot to escape Portugal unhindered after the Battle of Vimeiro, he was unable to contain his disgust. Although the inquiry on the Convention of Cintra eventually dismissed all charges against Wellesley, Philip Henry, a great duke admirer and young conservative MP, recorded in 1840 that Wellington complained of the "shabby fellows" who pressed their unfounded accusations against him with hypocritical, "fawning civility."[47]

Such obstacles and frustrations are narrated precisely because they prove the undaunted resilience of the man who had to—indeed was destined to—succeed. This typological narrative, in which the Iron subsumes the Duke, in Wellington's most famous sobriquet, the "Iron Duke," demonstrates that his most prized and enduring legacy is the hero's inextricable fusion with the myth of a uniquely English indomitability. As the *Morning Herald* argued, "Such characters as . . . Wellington . . . are thoroughly English. An avoidance of glitter and show, an indomitable perseverance, an unhesitating loyalty, and a constant reference to the dictates of duty."[48] In the person of Wellington, providence decrees what Europe's liberty demands. The anonymous poet of *The Fourteenth of September* says as much in a single couplet that reveals the eschatological impulse behind much of the Wellington mythmaking: "[Wellington] lived his mission to achieve; / Fulfilled the task by Heaven assigned him."[49] Maxwell's *Life* is characteristic of the moral imperative compelling all of these panegyrics. In that text, readers are entreated to "take a just pride" in Wellington and other ministers of George III's time; the predicaments confronted during the Napoleonic Wars confirmed "the resolution and constancy of those statesmen who triumphantly steered the United Kingdom through circumstances of extraordinary difficulty, and brought her to a high position among the nations."[50]

If the Victorians promoted simplicity and common sense as the touchstones of Wellington's character, panegyric—a form of testimonial employing a language of overstatement that is anything but simple and that resolutely discredits the common—is the medium through which the duke is made a laudatory subject after death, even in the professedly objective organs of the press. As public eulogies relying on deliberately elaborate encomium, panegyrics free their practitioners from conforming to the constraints of disinterestedness and balanced consideration that ideally characterize biographical discourse. "Ever mindful of [Wellington's] wonderful achievements," Walter May writes, with the implicit knowledge that his own panegyric enjoys generic license, wholly excluding contentious voices, "I have been constantly ready to extol his excellence." May concludes his pamphlet with an address to other potential, non-English panegyrists, inviting them to take up his subject and match the bravado of his own linguistic veneration. "I challenge any sage in Europe, deeply versed in his vernacular language," he states, "to carry his ideas to such sublimity and grandeur of expression as shall convey an adequate representation of the character of our incomparable Hero and Patriot."[51] May sets out to inspire what nationalist, hero-worshiping ideology eventually achieved: a world literature permanently immortalizing his hero.

One aspect of this immortalization was the ubiquitous enlistment of Wellington's image in a wide array of commemorative merchandise in the two-month hiatus between his death and funeral. As John Morley has observed of the Victorian funeral, "Sorrow was to provide a market that was to be well supplied with goods."[52] Wellington's funeral marked its place in history in part by rallying commodities and their advertisers in a way that had been heralded by the Great Exhibition. Hucksters, publishers, illustrators, and a burgeoning coalition of kitsch and novelty manufacturers all jumped at the chance to profit from the hero's passing. Chapter 4 investigates the market opened up by these entrepreneurs in an effort to better comprehend how liminality—that double threshold of space and time in which the duke's corpse was preserved to await interment—could be turned into various forms of profit, whether that meant hard returns from the sale of curios and souvenirs or the more evanescent cultural dividends derived from adding another illustrious name to the pantheon of English warrior heroes.

FOUR

The Waiting Game

Selling Wellington and Crowd Anxiety

A MERE two weeks after Wellington's death, the *Age*, a London
weekly, noted with some disdain that "every shop window from
Hammersmith to Bow [was] filled with scores on scores of pictures of the
late Duke—pictures of him at every age, in every dress, in every attitude,
and in every circumstance . . . a universal and bewildering array . . .
fling[ing] itself, as it were, in the faces of doubting purchasers."[1] For a
brief moment, it seemed, central London had been turned into a display
case for the advertisement and sale of Wellington imagery. In a supplement for early November, the *Illustrated London News* promised to contribute to this display in "a manner worthy of the event" by supplying
regular subscribers with a cornucopia of "large and magnificent sheet engravings"; included in a projected "Programme of the most important
Subjects chosen for Illustration" were no fewer than thirty-four pictures
directly related to the funeral ceremony itself (figure 4.1). Such advertising proved to be highly effective: one "indication of widespread . . . fascination with the Duke's funeral was the 'extreme and unprecedented' sales

FIGURE 4.1 *State Funeral of the Duke of Wellington, Illustrated London News,* 13 November 1852.

of copies of the *Illustrated London News,* amounting to a total of nearly two million for the numbers of 20 and 27 November."[2]

This sudden and omnipresent profusion of eclectic images evidently struck some Victorians as an effect of modernity, an exceptional and "bewildering" instance of the encroachment of the commodity upon national grieving. But remarkable as it was, it was not unprecedented. Stephen Behrendt has documented how the death of Princess Charlotte thirty-five years earlier—what Harriet Martineau called "the great historical event of 1817"[3]—resulted in a similar and equally astonishing array of commemorative images and artifacts, among them pieces of china, ceramics, metalwork, plate, textiles, prints, and sculpture. In death, Charlotte was resourcefully capitalized upon. Her posthumous commodification, however, like Wellington's after her, was distinctively modern in that it depended upon advances in the production and dissemination of goods that marked Britain's recent industrialization. As Behrendt observes,

> One of the inevitable consequences of the Industrial Revolution was just this sort of commoditizing of public events of all sorts, for that revolution set in motion complex cultural, economic and materialist forces that made it possible, in a way that it had never been before, for people to have a physical, material stake in events like Charlotte's death and the mourning ritual that followed. At the same time that the Industrial Revolution guaranteed an ever more rapidly increasing proliferation of physical goods, it assured that their prices would simultaneously fall, putting those goods within the reach of an ever hungrier consuming public.[4]

The *ILN*'s full-page advertisement for Wellington illustrations provides singular evidence of this "commoditizing of public events." Innovatively combining image and text in a moderately priced medium printed weekly on steam-driven presses, the illustrated newspaper invited consumers to possess the duke in the readily accessible form of the mass-produced image: "Items like . . . cheap memorial prints made it possible for . . . poorer citizens to participate in, rather than being shut out from . . . broadly community-oriented activities."[5] As memorial artifacts, the *ILN*'s "magnificent sheet engravings" were tangible objects upon which individual mourners could focus in the absence of the subject they commemorated.

Wellington's commodification was therefore a result of the increasing alliance between hero worship and commodity culture at midcentury. The engravings, sketches, and paintings of the duke that multiplied after his death tapped into the aspirations of a public that "yearned for hero-worship and sought the evidence of the titanic wherever it might be found."[6] Whereas the *ILN* enthusiastically appropriated the dead duke's image, profiting handsomely, the unillustrated *Age* maintained an attitude of incredulity toward the market for "scores on scores of pictures"—a market it was unwilling and apparently unable to either join or endorse.

Christopher Eimer puts the *Age*'s observations into perspective by echoing the periodical's language, pointing out that "the life and times of the first Duke of Wellington inspired many artists and caught the imagination of the public at large, for whom a bewildering variety of decorative art and objects were made. They catered for every taste and class of buyer and include paintings, sculpture and prints, as well as functional items in pottery, wood, and metal."[7] But it was Wellington's death, in particular, that was to initiate a truly astonishing explosion of memorabilia. Between 1852 and 1853, for example, at least forty-six different memorial coins and medals of the duke were struck and offered for sale, so that even today, Wellington medallic portraits are the most numerous of all personal medals in the British series.[8] And as the *Age* suggested, the ubiquitous Wellington portraits seemed to change the face of commercial London in the autumn of 1852: the duke peered out into the city's streets from "every shop window," a most pervasive revenant. These widely displayed pictures lent the dead hero a new, if transitory, public life.

Those ubiquitous pictures noted by the *Age,* however, were neither publicly sponsored nor permanent visual memorials. Rather, they were commodities produced for private consumption. They marked, in fact, the second mass reification of the duke in imagery and were reminiscent of the merchandise produced during the later stages of the peninsular campaign: "From 1810 to 1815 the British public demanded varied representations of [Wellington] on walls, snuff-boxes, tea services, fans, bells, door-stops, brooches, note-books, clocks, watches, barometers, and razors."[9] Whereas the Wellington curios and gadgets of the Napoleonic Wars transformed the glorious victories of the moment into a plebian vernacular, the posthumous, equally innovative merchandising took immediate advantage of eminent death by hastily fabricating a new market, that of the postmortem Wellington memento. This market may have had its roots in the earlier peninsular campaign souvenirs and the proliferation of Wellington caricatures by artists such as William Heath and John Doyle in the late 1820s and early 1830s, but its novelty lay in the fact that a startlingly broad assortment of memorial images of the duke was now readily available to anyone with some spare change.[10]

The *ILN*'s reproduction of Sir Thomas Lawrence's 1818 canvas *The Duke on Horseback* (figure 4.2) is an instance of high art brought to the multitudes. As a newspaper wood engraving of a steel-plate etching that

FIGURE 4.2 *Field-Marshall His Grace the Duke of Wellington*, after
Sir Thomas Lawrence, *Illustrated London News*, 18 September 1852.

traces its origin to the brush of the age's chief portraitist and past president of the Royal Academy, this instance of the image's mass dissemination shows that, in late 1852, any but the most penurious could readily
aspire to owning a replica of what one Lawrence critic called "the most
satisfactory, most worthy, and the noblest portrait of the Iron Duke that

exists," simply by purchasing a copy of the *ILN* for sixpence.[11] *The Duke on Horseback* is just one example of what Natalie Houston has called "the logic of the souvenir,"[12] wherein the public and the monumental are miniaturized, appropriated, and consumed by the individual subject. Victorian illustrated newspapers were in a unique position to mass-produce and sell such visual souvenirs, turning historical figures into portable and collectible "forms of cultural memory."[13] The *ILN*, in particular, advertising itself as "a complete record of all the events of the week . . . illustrated in a high style of art by wood-engravers of the first eminence, printed in a form convenient for binding,"[14] encouraged readers to preserve and display its pictures as bona fide, if proliferate, "art," through which "the eternal register of the pencil" gave "life and vigor and palpability" to history and its heroes.[15] Indeed, the *ILN* declared its eminent suitability for "the shelf—not shelved as we use the word despisingly, but in the sense of treasure-trove—picked up, garnished, and bound together as a fair ornament . . . as a library oracle to be consulted and referred to . . . for wisdom and history."[16] Properly cherished as an encyclopedia, the bound *ILN* actively participated in "the logic of the souvenir."

What the *Age* and Eimer call consumer "bewilderment" may, ultimately, be understood as a confusion about authenticity in the face of the overproduction of pictures and other such souvenirs: which images or relics really represent the dead duke? This question can be explored fruitfully only when it is reformulated to apprehend each picture as a representation incorporating various cultural and political subtexts. The vast majority of Wellington representations in the months following his death gestured unambiguously toward ideals of masculinity and soldierly heroism, but within this dominant imaginary, numerous less transparent themes are discernible. Advertising in the wake of Wellington was highly adept at picking up on these themes, amplifying and revising them in order to promote commodities that were to be imbued with heroic aura. Wellington's postmortem commodification intensified the debate about who the duke was and which products—books, pictures, medallions, statues—were to accurately represent his legacy.

By the time of the funeral, anyone perusing the advertising columns of the daily newspapers would have been directly faced with this debate as

Wellington's name and image were hawked in the marketplace of memorabilia. On the day before the procession, the *Morning Herald* promoted no fewer than ten funeral-related goods and services, among them: a ticket for the St. Paul's ceremony priced at one hundred guineas; a five-shilling print in tinted lithography of the funeral car; private viewings of T. J. Barker's picture of the meeting between Wellington and Prussian Field Marshal Gebbard Leberecht von Blücher at Waterloo; copies of John Barnett's song, "The Hero's Burial," for two shillings and sixpence; a Wellington brooch by W. H. Kerr and Company; and covered seats to view the procession from St. Mary-le-Strand Church.[17]

This last advertisement was perhaps the most notable, touching upon the funeral's capacity to generate enormous profits for the well-situated and enterprising entrepreneur: "A first floor in Piccadilly cost £60; some with bay windows cost a hundred guineas. The *Observer* calculated—and this was thought a low estimate—that £80,000 changed hands for seats."[18] A dominant feature in illustrations of the parade route, the temporary stands for paying spectators were installed on all the major London arteries through which the procession passed. "Along the intended route of the procession," the *Morning Herald* wrote on the day before the funeral, "every tenement which has the least pretensions to obtaining a view of the *cortége* [*sic*] is let, parcelled out into the greatest number of seats, and sub-let again. Coming east from Apsley House, the scaffoldings erected against the house fronts become gradually more numerous, until, as in St. James's-street and Pall-Mall, they form almost one continuous balcony running from window to window."[19] *ILN* readers were offered a view of the procession as it marched westward along Pall Mall (figure 4.3), with four of that dignified street's clubhouses clearly visible from the left: the colonnaded United Services, the Athenaeum, the Travelers', and the Reform. Most conspicuous, however, was the transformation of these edifices by the scaffolding of the viewers' stands, which converted imposing piles into background supports for onlookers, whose own social status was denominated by the height to which they could ascend.

There were occasional remonstrances against this brazen spectacularization and commodification of the heroic dead. The *Scotsman,* for example, refused to doff its nationalist hat by genuflecting before Wellington's grave

FIGURE 4.3 *The Procession in Pall-Mall, Illustrated London News*, 11 December 1852.

and instead sneered at the English propensity to turn mourning into profit making and the procession itself into pure spectacle:

> A great variety of people seize on such an event as an opportunity for making profit or popularity, and do not always conduct their operations with unimpeachable good taste. Another outlet has been afforded to the torrent of panegyric and of anecdote which ran itself to the dregs two months ago. . . . In the motives which drew so many tens of thousands to London this week, there was doubtless much of mere vulgar sight-seeing—no small proportion of them went, not to express grief or to pay honour, but simply to see a procession.[20]

There is something disingenuous about the *Scotsman*'s attempt to play arbiter, as if it had special access to the genuine emotional states of spectators and was somehow above the fascination with "vulgar" show that had also been castigated by numerous clergymen. For Edinburgh's self-declared *"Political and Literary Journal,"* however, the gorgeous funeral only verified for nationalist Scots that the English were prone to overplay their own importance through praise for representative military heroes; the *Scotsman* therefore damned Wellington with faint praise, concluding that "to the copious, and eloquent, and generally concurring testimonies borne . . . by our contemporaries, there is little that we feel either called on or able to add."[21]

The *Scotsman*'s virtuous imprecations against spectacular self-glorification, however, also need to be contextualized within the framework of an understandable ressentiment. In its issue for 25 September 1852, the paper deplored the fact that Scottish soldier-heroes were consistently ignored by history, a result of chauvinism on the part of the English, who appeared to willfully forget the military successes of the Scots against Edward II in the early fourteenth century. The duke's death became an occasion for the *Scotsman* to introduce a third term into the conventional opposition between two martial titans, Wellington and Napoleon: "Nothing but the rarest combination of the finest moral and intellectual gifts, such as it would be mockery to attribute to Napoleon, and would be flattery to bestow on Wellington, could have enabled Robert Bruce to do what he did."[22]

In this clever denigration of nineteenth-century heroes, Bruce emerged as the consummate protagonist, an incorruptible genius whose qualities subsumed and overawed those of latter-day champions. Wellington's death and its exaggerated celebration formed the grist for a wholesale attack on English bigotry.

The *Scotsman's* criticisms were leveled primarily at English spectators, with their predilection to compose thoughtless "torrents of panegyric" in honor of a man they elected to view as a representative of their highest accomplishments and best moral selves. In a similar vein, funeral reformers—generally referred to simply as ecclesiologists—had throughout the 1840s expressed their disapproval of excessive and, perhaps more pertinently, expensive pagan ritual in favor of a simpler Christian piety. Although eventually successful in stirring up popular opposition to the "cost . . . magisterial formality . . . [and] meaningless etiquette" of the early Victorian funeral, ecclesiological protests did nothing to dampen appreciation for Wellington's procession, which met with surprisingly little resistance.[23] On the whole, the funeral and Wellington merchandising was readily tolerated as an intelligible succession to other forms of moneymaking that had come to be perceived as both natural and commendable earlier in the century. Mass production and the "invention" of industrial exhibitions to display its proliferating goods laid the groundwork for the opening of a historically unique Wellington market:

> One could buy "cypress hatbands," or "a mourning head-dress, suitable for wearing in the Cathedral"—this latter was especially designed not to impede the view, as would a bonnet. Accessories were not limited to mourning wear; a tailor's firm recommended a life preserver for everybody on the 18th, and an optician his "portable perspective glasses, for viewing objects within the distance of a mile, so extensively patronized on this occasion." . . . Souvenirs and relics were popular. . . . A great variety appeared for sale. . . . Poetry poured in profusion into the ears of the public. As early as October 2nd the second edition of "A Dirge for Wellington" by Martin Tupper was advertised at 6d; or one could buy "His Pilgrimage Is Ended" for 2s, or "A Great Man Fallen" for 6d, the latter a sermon preached in St. Peter's Church, Yoxell.[24]

On the one hand, Wellington's death generated an advertising campaign for conventional mourning paraphernalia. This predictable enterprise sought to profit from outfitting mourners according to the governing codes of funereal etiquette, wherein "the display of feeling . . . became a necessary part of the social equipment of every polite person."[25] The *Age* even partook in a debate about the expression of appropriate sentiment by assuring its female readers that no special apparel was required before the day of the procession: women in "considerable doubt . . . with reference to the description of mourning to be worn at the funeral" were heartened by the paper's assertion that "we are in a position to state, upon authority, that no mourning is to be worn except on the day of the funeral."[26] The public burial of a great man did not require the usual observances of the funeral week on the part of most spectators, and it saved female mourners in particular from the expense and discomfort of wearing crepe for a prolonged period of time.

On the other hand, another more extraordinary mode of advertising materialized in the months following Wellington's death. Goods and services wholly unrelated to the deceased were suddenly pitched in a way that borrowed from the charisma of Wellington; the duke's name was invoked to sanction commodities (life preservers and perspective glasses) to which he had no connection or to which the most nebulous of associations was concocted. Wellington's funeral was an opportunity to advertise the qualities and virtues of commodities that, prior to the event of death, had no affiliation whatsoever with the individual.

The duke's name, for example, was literally patched onto common household wares, ornamenting objects in a way that contributed nothing to their usefulness but lent them symbolic meaning ludicrously in excess of their pedestrian materiality. Before Wellington had been dead for three weeks, the *Leeds Mercury* advertised, at £3 for four yards, "Damask Tablecloths and napkins, containing the equestrian statue of the Duke of Wellington, encircled by his Heraldic Orders, and bordered by the Rose, Shamrock, and Thistle."[27] Again, this dramatic abridgment of Wellington's charisma exhibited the logic of the souvenir, as the "miniature attempt[ed] to signify the gigantic by compressing the public sphere into the narrow compass of small objects designed for private consumption."[28]

The Wellington napkin-as-memento was overburdened with significance: the death of the hero gave rise to the collectible.

The newspapers themselves also profited substantially during the period between Wellington's death and funeral. In their capacity to capitalize on the hero's death, one witnessed the incredible resourcefulness and the strategic fertility of the media as it drews its narratives out to such an extent that it seemed they would never end.

This drawing out was practiced with great acuity by the Victorian press. The ongoing success of any periodical depends on its capacity to maintain a readership, which is accomplished in part through consistency of production (the paper must appear regularly) and the promise of formal continuity (the paper must have a readily identifiable, material presence— a "character"). As Margaret Beetham remarks, the newspaper

> must be read diachronically along the time line of its production as well as synchronically in terms of the single issue or number. Since the periodical depends on ensuring that the readers continue to buy each number as it comes out, there is a tendency in the form not only to keep reproducing elements which have been successful but also to link each number to the next. This can be done through running a series of articles, through constant reference to past and future issues, through advertising, through readers' letters and through serialization. . . . The form is, therefore, not only characteristically self-referring but is by definition open-ended and resistant to closure.[29]

The last two observations about self-referentiality and resistance to closure deserve particular attention with regard to coverage of Wellington's death. Both functions were animated at midcentury by external factors that would have initially appeared debilitating but ultimately contributed to the prosperity of the press: the significant delay between the death and interment resulted in a protracted series of published suppositions about the date, scale, and cultural implications of the duke's state funeral, an ongoing series of hypotheses that enhanced continuity between issues, stimulated curiosity, and cultivated new readers.

Newspapers turned speculation about the funeral and procession into textual capital. In the process, each competed with its contemporaries by referring to its own uniqueness and superiority in terms of access to information and quality of presentation. But this information took time to disseminate. The *Leeds Mercury* was not alone in observing that "one of the first questions that must be decided is the proper place for [Wellington's] interment, and upon this point there already exists much speculation."[30] The *Morning Chronicle,* too, noted that "it has been suggested that [Wellington] should be interred in St. Paul's by the side of Nelson, but it has also been suggested that, having been a statesman as well as a soldier, his remains should be interred at Westminster Abbey."[31] Wellington's double career as both a military commander and an influential politician complicated the decision. By the late eighteenth century, as Clare Gittings has demonstrated, a plan had been developed "to institutionalize hero worship by turning St. Paul's Cathedral into a national 'Valhalla,' a resting place for Britain's heroes, to be commemorated by neo-classical statues."[32] Such institutionalization, however, was never rigorously implemented: soldier-heroes continued to be interred at Westminster along with the nation's artists and legislators, whereas St. Paul's lacked the credentials of a true Valhalla, a hall assigned exclusively to those who die in battle. Nelson might have fit the criteria, but Wellington's death in old age made him an inappropriate candidate. In late September, although the *Chronicle* felt "authorized to state that the funeral of the late Duke . . . will be a public one," it was also forced to admit that "the arrangements respecting it are not yet definitively settled."[33]

As a weekly member of the provincial press, however, a paper such as the *Mercury* was somewhat handicapped when it came to resources, circulation, and influence. Whereas "such newspapers as the *Times* or, increasingly, the Sunday papers, circulated widely throughout Britain, and . . . magazines emanating from London were read in homes and public institutions across the country,"[34] the independent function of provincials at midcentury was largely confined to reporting local news. "Provincial newspapers received parliamentary and foreign news when the London papers arrived," one scholar has observed, "and were thus, willy-nilly, restricted to a role as recounters of local affairs and second-hand reporters of what the London papers had already said."[35] The same page of the *Mercury* that commented on speculation about Wellington's interment, therefore, made up for what it lacked in reliable coverage by quoting heavily from London periodicals, particularly the *Times* (on the duke's personal habits), an unspecified "evening journal" (on the supposed contents of Wellington's will), and the *Sporting Magazine* (on the appearance and character of Copenhagen, Wellington's favorite charger). Leeds readers were also treated to quoted extracts from a memorial sermon preached at the Scottish National Church in Covent Garden.

Through these selective interpolations, the *Mercury* stayed in the game, turning to its advantage the fact that telegraphic communication had made it possible for news to arrive "almost instantaneously from the four corners of the world, and could be reported almost simultaneously in London and the remotest provincial town."[36] Nevertheless, this paper had nothing original to add to the Wellingtoniana in the first days after the death. Not until the funeral had concluded did the *Leeds Mercury* give its assessment of the proceedings, calling the procession "a spectacle of overpowering interest and grandeur" and throwing its hat into the ring of panegyrical competition by asserting that "it is not easy to say what honours could be in excess, to testify to the gratitude of universal England for services so inestimable, in peace as well as war, as those of Wellington."[37]

As the *Morning Chronicle* noted nearly two months after the *Mercury*'s initial report on Wellington's death, "From the day of the Duke's death, masses of information and discussion as to his life and character occupied whole pages of the newspapers. Indeed, the amount of journalistic, military, political, biographical, and anecdotal matter . . . offered to the public, was without measure or example."[38] In the *Illustrated London News*, as the advertisement in figure 4.1 shows, these "masses of information" sometimes took otiose and bizarre forms; the publication of arcane pictorial intelligence, even if its representational accuracy was dubious, gave this illustrated weekly an edge in the increasingly stiff competition for readers. For example, the *ILN* published numerous large engravings of the duke's coffin, his various chargers, and his many insignia (batons, orders, and ceremonial plate). Admitting that its "admiration of [Wellington's] character seems excessive," the *ILN* nevertheless promised to provide its readers with "every interesting feature and characteristic" about the hero's life and death.[39]

Hence, the *ILN* reproduced another Lawrence portrait of Wellington's mother and commented extensively upon its merits, rationalizing this foray into the world of art criticism by declaring that, while deploring the loss of the great duke, "every circumstance connected with the family hearth in which he was reared becomes invested with deep poetic interest."[40] The *ILN* also gave over a full, three-columned page to reproductions of Wellington family autographs, suggesting that "public attention, which occupies itself with even the most trifling details relative to departed greatness," must take an interest in these signatures, especially in the duke's own "uniform, aristocratical, and very legible" one.[41] By attributing to its reading public the demand for such esoteric "information," the *ILN* glossed the reality of its own predicament, a predicament that nonetheless offered opportunity for higher sales: it had to fill space and maintain interest in the duke while elaborate and time-consuming funeral preparations were being made.

Obsessive attention to such details, then, was a resourceful form of stalling. Newspapers were forced into a state of deferral, supplementing their columns with general conjecture, but there was never any threat of absolute paralysis even in the immediate wake of Wellington's death. Rather, what the *Morning Chronicle* was to call the "blank" left by the duke's demise presented an initial challenge to the dailies and weeklies as they scrambled to convert the fact of Wellington's passing into "news"—communications that were "up-to-the-minute, full, worldwide, and above all true"[42]—while working under the limitations engendered by a lack of hard information. If "the relationship to time is the central characteristic of the periodical,"[43] then in the *Chronicle's* effusive but garbled tribute to Wellington the day after his death, one sees the traces of that newspaper's rushed attempt to produce something newsworthy for the morning deadline—the paper's ultimate prerogative, which gave no quarter when demanding fresh intelligence. The "blank," in other words, had double reference, describing not only the nation's loss in Wellington but also the paper void that required filling:

> Yet the blank which has been made . . . the blow which has been struck at our councils, both of peace and of war—its infinite social significance—its vast civil importance—its deep emotional interest to every British heart—cannot but render us, for the moment, less willing than we usually are to treat at once, formally and historically,

the life and the reputation of the illustrious man who has just left us. . . . In the immediate anguish of the bereavement . . . we naturally concentrate the mournful tenor of our thoughts around the still thrilling catastrophe.[44]

This statement is prevarication worked up into unintentional self-caricature, a seeming hybridization of genres in which reportage collides with panegyric and deferential "unwillingness" serves as an excuse for temporary incapacity. If Wellington's death was disconcerting, it was scarcely an acute setback to the councils of state. Wellington had been disengaged from active political life since 1846, when he resigned as leader of the Opposition for the House of Lords. Arguably, the duke's star had permanently declined as early as 1834, when he gave up the ministry to join Robert Peel's government without portfolio. If it was not, in any meaningful sense of the phrase, a *thrilling catastrophe,* however, Wellington's death was to become—and the distinction between already constituting and eventually becoming is an important one, elided by the *Chronicle*—a matter of considerable if not "infinite social significance."

The *Morning Chronicle*'s accolades for Wellington might surprise present-day readers, who would expect a newspaper to cite such praise from the deceased's political colleagues and admirers rather than present it as the periodical's ardent conviction. Leading articles in Victorian newspapers, however, generally provided opinion that was, according to Edward Royle, "erudite, outraged, biased, self-righteous and combative according to the mood, the material and the circumstance"; when seeking to gauge "the development of policy within the group represented by the editor and the paper," these are the commentaries to which researchers first look.[45] And the *Chronicle*'s embellishment was complemented by numerous other tributes published in the British press immediately after Wellington's death. For the *Times,* the duke would be the figure recalled "when men in after times look back to the annals of England for examples of energy and public virtue among those who have raised this country to her station on the earth."[46] For *John Bull,* Wellington stood "distinguished, not only unsurpassed or unrivaled, but unequaled."[47]

If, however, these initial plaudits seem to have made news an exercise in sycophancy, they did so not simply to advertise the papers' allegiance to

Wellington's brand of conservatism, although as Royle notes, such eulogies said something significant about the *Times*'s and *John Bull*'s political dispositions. Adulation also temporarily substituted for news, creating a framework for the biographical and pictorial commemorations that were to follow under subsequent headings such as "The Duke of Wellington as Administrator of the Army," "The Duke of Wellington and the Peerage," and "The Duke of Wellington at Waterloo." Wellington panegyric in the press can thus be situated within the exigencies of periodicals publication in the nineteenth century, a mode of production that created inevitable time lags as reporters, illustrators, compositors, press operators, and distributors did their jobs. Although deadlines were inflexible, they were confronted with an ingenuity requisite of publications that relied on such labor- and time-consuming tasks as wood-block engraving and letterpress compositing.

The *Morning Chronicle,* therefore, made a virtue of necessity. Just as the "infinite" breach left by the duke's death was promptly filled in by advertisements for Wellington memorabilia, so the *Chronicle*'s apparent crossover from measured opinion to unadulterated praise helped it stay abreast of rivals: panegyric was the only narrative option available during that brief space of time between the "thrilling catastrophe" itself and the issue for 20 September, by which point the newspaper had rallied its resources enough to comment on Wellington's powers of memory, his unostentatious donations to charity, and the grief of his favorite chef ("even the French cook, overlooking Waterloo and his Grace's indifference to the science of gastronomy, mourns for his death"[48]). The same number included front-page advertisements for prints of Count D'Orsay's portrait of the duke; two special numbers of the *ILN* promised "interesting engravings, illustrating a complete life of the Duke," and a reprint of the *Times*'s earlier "Memoir of the Duke."

Evidently, the blank was short-lived. The language used to describe it in the *Chronicle* passage quoted earlier is also a language of immanence that invested in the death the qualities of a prodigious and incomparable event. The preeminence ascribed to the death, however, like that attributed to Wellington, should be comprehended as an effect of repeated narrative inscriptions, cumulative retellings over the course of time: the magnitude of the event "remain[ed] a product of the discourse that surrounded it,"[49] so that the *Morning Chronicle*'s perception of the "vast importance" of the duke's death actually inaugurated the process by which it achieved cultural significance.

The importance attached to Wellington's death also functioned as an apologia for his extravagant funeral. Poets and members of the Anglican clergy argued that costly funeral arrangements were compatible with "that high and honourable position in the world, which was ably and advantageously occupied by [the] lamented general and statesman."[50] The memorial literature, however, also tended to rigorously insulate Wellington from pejorative anecdote, a point that returns us to an earlier observation: the Wellington marketed in the months after his death was an imago or phantasy figure expurgated of any biographical appraisal that failed to contribute to his ultimate deification. In this sense, what the English press, in particular, did *not* say is of more interest than what it published.

Punch, for example, although never an admirer of Wellington's politics, remained uncharacteristically silent on such issues on the occasion of his death, alluding instead to his supposed affection for children in a memorial poem in its number for 18 September 1852, wherein Wellington was represented as a man of internal warmth: "Underneath the armour of his breast / Were springs of tenderness"; "children climbed his knees, and made his arms their nest."[51] Such recollections were not only acceptable to the English press, they were essential to an ideological exchange between newspapers—self-appointed representatives of "the voice of the people" —and their readers, those the *Illustrated London News* christened its "real, faithful, and influential patrons," for whom the paper "kept the purity of [its] columns inviolate and supreme."[52] This exchange was a transaction between apparent confederates (on the one hand, "the respectable families of England," on the other, a paper displaying an "adherence to those undisputed maxims of morals and Christianity upon which all good men are agreed"[53]) that fashioned Wellington into an emblem of virtuous living capable of enticing those who saw in the duke a covetable paragon of English integrity. The *Morning Chronicle* contrasted Wellington with Nelson and found in the former a more estimable nature: "The Hero of Waterloo had neither the splendid weaknesses nor the warm emotional spirit of the Hero of Trafalgar. But the Duke's was a higher, a more com-

plete, and a nobler character."[54] Whereas Wellington conscientiously fulfilled his duties as husband to the indiscreet and quick-tempered Kitty,
Nelson separated from Frances Nisbet to form a liaison with the disreputable Emma Hamilton.

By seeking to impose a uniform probity on the way that Wellington's
legacy was narrated, newspapers were doing much the same thing as the
funeral's organizers attempted during October and November 1852: they
sought to ensure the decorum and orderliness of commemorative activities. London's shop windows and the columns of the nation's periodicals
may have featured a riot of advertised pictures and objects immediately
after Wellington's death, but the procession and interment were to be a
model of sobriety and good order. The funeral was not only to reflect the
status of the man it celebrated, it was also to function in after times as an
advertisement for the Victorian capacity to effectively organize and display. It was, in short, to repeat the success of the Great Exhibition.

Several newspapers were anxious to ensure the funeral's success, and
they used the interlude between Wellington's death and funeral to exhort
would-be spectators to practice restraint. The solicitude with which the
press anticipated the obsequies divulged a peculiar tension: popular reverence for a deified hero threatened to degenerate into unruliness. Those
"incessant streams of persons," as a correspondent for the *Leeds Mercury*
called them, "flowing along the streets from day-break nearly to midnight
towards Chelsea Hospital" to view the duke's coffin during the lying in
state,[55] became in the minds of some observers an increasingly ominous
tide, a confluence of indistinguishable and unpredictable strangers flood-
ing London's West End as the day for Wellington's procession drew near.
Apprehension about the funeral indicated how acutely aware many members of the Victorian middle and professional classes were of the fine line
separating orderly festivity from outright pandemonium. More important,
as uneasiness about the gathering and mixing of a potentially capricious,
socially heterogenous mass devolved into congratulatory tributes on the
good order (if not good taste) exhibited by everyone involved in the procession and burial, it became obvious that the crowd had functioned as
a successful "test-case," as John Plotz has called it, "for the limits of the
public sphere," since it also served as a "vigorous . . . rival to many of

the [Victorian] era's most ingrained assumptions about the segregation of classes and the segmentation of public spheres."[56]

As the *Times* wistfully noted, however, the delay between death and funeral was not calculated to guarantee the "quiet and orderly behaviour of all." Whereas the *Times* suggested simply that it was "but reasonable that all persons . . . should endeavour . . . to maintain order"—a "caution for rich and poor . . . for those who have paid their guineas for sittings on any of the numerous scaffoldings . . . as for the humblest classes who are endeavouring to maintain their places upon the pavement's edge"[57]—the *Morning Chronicle* appeared to repress by denying the possibility of public commotion, predicting that the funeral would "be a household word for the remainder of the century—it must not be coupled with any regret."[58] At least one provincial paper commented in some detail on the "suffering of the crowd" in front of Chelsea Hospital, too eager to admire the ornamented hall in which Wellington's catafalque was on display: "Steam . . . went up in one dense cloud from the panting struggling mass . . . and when the barrier was attained . . . their flushed faces, bathed with perspiration, testified to the extent of the exhaustion to which they had been reduced."[59] Members of the press seemed eager to scent out proofs that anxiety was warranted, even if their worst fears were never realized.

Such intimations of disaster were, in part, a residue of eighteenth-century apprehensions about that increasingly vigorous and threatening body of popular resistance, the crowd turned mob. As the Gordon riots of 1780 had demonstrated, a well-organized, relatively orderly crowd could quickly degenerate into "indiscriminate orgies of drunkenness, arson, and pickpocketing."[60] Although outbursts of such violence and destruction reached a crescendo in the 1790s, the possibility of mobbish disturbance continued to haunt the national consciousness, as obsessive interest in the 1848 Jacobin eruptions on the Continent proved—recent revolutionary activity, as I have already noted, recollected by mourners of the duke with some trepidation now that their counterrevolutionary hero was dead.

Still, judging by press coverage, Wellington's aura was preserved as a sort of totem against French revolutionary influence and any disturbances that might be provoked by a capricious crowd that included a large number of working-class spectators. "England, Heaven be praised! was never more tranquil than at this moment," the *Morning Chronicle* exclaimed shortly after news of the duke's death, recalling deprecatingly John Russell's Whig ministry and Wellington's role in planning London's defenses against the Chartist petitioners: "But considering who were ministers on the 10th of April, 1848, may not the position of the country now be in part attributed to the admirable preventive and precautionary measures taken four years and a half ago by the Duke of Wellington?"[61] The *Chronicle's* rhetorical question encapsulated an attitude common to the English press in its commemoration of Wellington. The aged duke was as effective in quelling radical fervor as he had been in destroying a self-proclaimed revolutionary emperor. Surely, this line of eulogizing intimated, the reputation of such a man must not be sullied with opprobrious behavior at his funeral.

It was Queen Victoria who provided one of the most ingenuous but nonetheless telling expressions of relief regarding the waiting period's conclusion with what she regarded as a resoundingly successful pageant. In this respect, the monarch played a fitting role as the nation's gracious arbiter, seemingly incognizant of any dissension but hyperbolic in her praise for a job well done. A letter of 23 November 1852 to the queen's Belgian uncle, Leopold, appears mildly ironic in retrospect, a double exclamation of regret and applause that contrasts sharply with her despairing silence and retirement from public life after another famously solemnized Victorian death, that of her own husband some nine years later:

> You will have heard from your children and from Charles how very touching the ceremony both in and out of doors was on the 18th. The behaviour of the millions assembled has been the topic of general admiration, and the foreigners have all assured me that they never could have believed *such* a number of people could have shown such feeling, such respect, for *not* a sound was heard! I cannot say *what* a deep and *wehmtühige* [*sic*] impression it made on me! It was a beautiful sight. In the Cathedral it was much more touching still! The dear old Duke! he is an irreparable loss![62]

There is an affability, a discomfiting pleasure discernible in this passage, indicating that Victoria was already exhibiting a tendency to derive morbid satisfaction from celebrating the deaths of others.

Victoria can be usefully apprehended as a kind of barometer in extremis for the much touted Victorian love of exaggerated death ritual and superlative eulogy—modes of celebration that were not to be equaled after Wellington's funeral. By the time of Prince Albert's death in 1861 or Victoria's own public death procession forty years later, the spectacular and prolonged festival that characterized Wellington's laying to rest had become dated and inappropriate. Whereas the 1851 Great Exhibition proved to be a novel spectacle that inspired ever more elaborate and grander "international" exhibitions (Paris staged no fewer than five such "great occasions" between 1855 and 1900, and Philadelphia's massive 1876 centenary exhibition was itself outdone by Chicago's huge World's Columbian Exposition in 1893), Albert's death by typhoid fever was mourned in a comparatively intimate ceremony that displayed little of the sumptuousness of Wellington's funeral and took only nine days to plan and consummate. Victoria's own obsessive engagement with "the rituals and trappings of [Albert's] loss, expanding upon them to the point where she exhausted her subjects' capacity to enjoy or sympathize with the performance,"[63] substituted, in large part, for the duke's very public mourning. And the rapid transportation of the queen's body from Osborne House to Victoria station, expediting her entombment at Frogmore only twelve days after her death, indicated that the termination of the Victorian era coincided with the passing of protracted death ceremonies for the exalted of the nation.

Like the Great Exhibition before it, therefore, Wellington's state funeral functioned as a kind of social litmus test, only its glory was not to be emulated. As Victoria concluded, anxieties about serious disruption had, in the end, been unnecessary. Just as working-class visitors to the Crystal Palace "proved to be every bit as docile as the middle-class crowd . . . no longer look[ing] like the indigenous ally of the class that had rocked Europe in 1848" but functioning instead as "just another segment of the market,"[64] so spectators of the duke's procession mollified the press by behaving, by and large, with patience and sobriety. "Words are, we feel, completely powerless to convey anything like a just idea of a demonstration so marvelous," a *Times* editor was able to expound the day after the funeral. "On no occasion in modern times has such a concourse of people been gathered together, and never probably has the sublimity which is expressed by the presence of the masses been so transcendently displayed."[65]

Such broadly gratifying rhetoric congratulated Victorian readers on the success of the state funeral, which was, in the end, an event that had to induce the proper deportment of all classes. The *Times*'s happy diagnosis, however, quickly became a pervasive refrain that eventually sold to future historians the idea of Wellington's procession as an organizational coup unique in nineteenth-century Britain. Harry Garlick, who comments on the "elaborate and intensive preparation" undertaken for the funeral, finds it "gratifying to report that the entire populace who witnessed this event were sufficiently involved emotionally to discipline their own conduct and order."[66] Garlick echoes the perceptions of the Victorian press. A day after the *Times* concluded its reportage of the funeral, the *Illustrated London News* reported "in strong terms of commendation, the admirable conduct of the public, on all parts of the line. The police conducted themselves with courtesy, and were obeyed without a murmur."[67] Lord Palmerston, who took part in the procession, noted in his journal the "immense numbers of spectators" who kept "perfect order."[68] Marie Maurice wrote of "the reverent conduct of the million and a half persons . . . gathered together" to honor Wellington, "a grand witness to the feeling of national and universal sorrow which had drawn them together."[69] So, although there were moments of initial confusion (Richard Wellesley, Wellington's grandson, received a letter from his mother prior to the funeral in which she complained about being "quite in the dark as to our place of meeting on the morning of the 18th, whether . . . at the Horse Guards, Apsley House, or Chelsea"[70]), a general assessment was that things went off with hardly a hitch.

Good behavior at the procession despite its deferment equipped Victorian commentators with seeming proof that an armistice between classes had been achieved after the alarms of 1848. Although the postponement of finality led one newspaper to comment on "a restless anxiety [that] seemed to pervade the public mind, as if the occurrence of some great catastrophe might possibly be involved in the result,"[71] this was an observation made with the benefit of hindsight: the remark was part of a general, post-funeral euphoria that identified earlier anxieties in order to show that, in retrospect, they were groundless. As Victoria concluded, the British crowds comprised a subject of "general admiration," especially to foreigners. Once consummated, the funeral came to evoke the image of peace-loving Britons, a quiescent and civil people.

Delay, therefore, ultimately functioned as reprieve. Further, it offered numerous entrepreneurs the opportunity to make some quick money, while benefiting a wide range of artisans, merchants, and artists—the carpenters, for example, who built seating tiers in St. Paul's, the City of London Gas Company workers who laid six thousand gas lights in the cathedral, the suppliers of velvet and crepe for drapery at Chelsea Hospital—whose industry was compensated through the £80,000 of public money spent on the funeral. Chapter 5 revisits the scene of the procession and funeral, in the process examining the appropriateness of the obsequies as a reflection and affirmation of Wellington's personal and public legacy.

FIVE

Obsequies and Sanctification

W ELLINGTON'S common sense and supposed love for the simple life were not, in the end, to result in a funeral that reflected the continence of his habits. Once the duke's body was formally taken into the possession of the Crown, a guard of honor was placed around the coffin as it lay at Walmer, where more than ten thousand people viewed the casket as it awaited conveyance to London for the official lying in state. The coffin was transported to Chelsea on 10 November by hearse and train in the middle of the night in order to prevent large crowds from gathering to watch the penultimate procession of the hero's corpse. The Great Hall of Chelsea Hospital was laboriously redecorated, draped from ceiling to floor with shrouds of black cloth that blocked the sun so that the subdued light of enormous candles could create a suitably somber atmosphere. A long, covered passage, lined with banners representing Wellington's many military victories, led to an anteroom containing officers of the Brigade of Foot Guards, dressed in crepe and holding reversed arms. In the death chamber itself, the coffin was covered with crimson velvet and rested on

FIGURE 5.1 *The Lying in State of the Late Duke of Wellington*, 1852. © The Royal Hospital Chelsea.

a bier mantled in black velvet; at its foot were suspended all of Wellington's honors (batons, chains, medals, and orders). Around the dais, more guards were stationed on raised platforms. "The whole effect was theatrical, eccentric, powerful and imperially pagan; it compelled admiration" for the two hundred thousand people who filed past the bier.[1] A large colored print of this scene, depicting Queen Victoria's visit to the lying in state, still hangs in the Great Hall of Chelsea Hospital, a visual testament to the seventeenth-century edifice's finest moment (figure 5.1).

On 11 and 12 November, viewing of the coffin was restricted to royalty, peers, members of Parliament, and the military elite. The public was admitted without restriction for five days, from 13 to 17 November, although the deaths of two working-class women, Sarah Bean and Charlotte Cook, crushed against barricades erected outside the hospital as overeager crowds surged against the building on the first day of the lying in state, convinced authorities that entrance had to be more carefully monitored and disciplined. Early on the morning of 18 November, the coffin was removed to the parade ground of the Horse Guards near St. James's Park, the rallying point for the procession. Perched atop a colossal funeral car specially designed for it, the coffin was to become for some hours the ponderously moving nucleus of a ritual that ended with "the funeral service itself in the cathedral church of our city, the centre and navel as it were of that metropolis which is itself the centre of the world" and whose mourners were privileged to witness "the lowering of the hero's mortal remains to their last resting-place, beneath the central cross of England's central sanctuary."[2] If simplicity was one of Wellington's most acclaimed traits, *centrality* became a catchword for the funeral, an elaborate exercise in ideological concentration. Following in the wake of the Great Exhibition, Wellington's procession and burial guaranteed London's rank as the hub of the world, at least as far as Londoners themselves were concerned.

The temporary focal point of this metropolitan world center was the car itself (figure 5.2). It was designed in the remarkably short period of three weeks by the new Governmental Department of Practical Art, an agency that had been formed to help with the planning of the exhibition. The story of the funeral car, in fact, has several affinities with that of the earlier project. Under the watchful eye of Prince Albert, the services of Henry Cole were again called upon; with the expert help of designers Richard Redgrave and Gottfried Semper, Cole attempted to address Albert's recommendation that "the funeral car should not only be a symbol of English military strength and statesmanship, but also an expression of all the efforts of Victorian art."[3] The result of this ambitious endeavor was an II-ton, 6-wheeled, £11,000 "relic from a past age"[4]—a "figure out of the great Baroque pageants,"[5] displaying a plethora of symbolic reminders of Wellington's military victories. Although Harry Garlick has suggested that the ducal car resembled an early railway carriage on which Wellington's body was the singular "passenger,"[6] it is more tenable to appreciate its design as a derivation from examples of Roman victory chariots as imagined by prominent Renaissance artists.[7] Andrea Mantegna's well-known, nine-panel painting *Triumphs of Caesar,* for example, commissioned by the Gonzaga family of Mantua in the 1480s, portrays an official entrance in which the celebrants' focus is on an ornately carved, absurdly bulky conveyance strikingly similar to Wellington's funeral car, a fitting vehicle for Caesar

FIGURE 5.2 *The Duke of Wellington's Funeral Car,* Illustrated London News, 20 November 1852.

as he returns from victory over the Gauls. Mantegna's painted chariot and Cole's monstrous car are both overt expressions of admiration for Roman paradigms of monumentality; the latter seems to belong more properly to the age of the great triumphal processions than to the nineteenth century.[8]

The car did little to enhance the image of nineteenth-century art, although it cultivated a voluptuous confusion visually, the result of too many chefs at the broth. Anachronistic in design, the car met with some fierce criticism; it "appeared somewhat out of date to the more progressive contemporaries of Morris and Ruskin, particularly when it was literally loaded with details only intelligible to the student of classical archaeology."[9] Two days after the procession, the *Examiner* complained that it "had been for some days sedulously informed that the funeral car was a miracle of taste in all its parts, but certainly the entire effect of it was that of a gaudy, unwieldy, lumbering machine."[10] Thomas Carlyle agreed with this judgment and was, if anything, more vituperative in his condemnation of the car, the passing of which he watched from a rooftop in Fleet Street: "Of all the objects I ever saw," Carlyle recorded in his personal journal, the car was "the abominably ugliest, or nearly so . . . an incoherent huddle of expensive palls, flags, sheets and gilt emblems and cross poles." This "vile *ne plus ultra* of Cockneyism" could not be reconciled with Carlyle's earlier hero worship of the graceful, aged duke.[11]

The car fared no better in the critical judgment of master political diarist Charles Greville. His *Memoirs* articulated nicely the aforementioned tension between simplicity as an admirable trait of heroic character and a celebratory extravagance inappropriate to its commemoration. Wellington's "perfect simplicity of character" differentiated the Englishman from his military and moral opponent Napoleon Bonaparte, "who, with more genius and fertility of invention, was the Slave of his own passions, unacquainted with moral restraint."[12] Wellington's car was a second example of moderation scorned: it was "tawdry, cumbrous, and vulgar."[13] Whereas Paxton's Crystal Palace was the ideal container for midcentury commodities, a form that perfectly complemented its content(s) so that entering it was "an almost hallucinatory experience: you felt overpowered by sweetness and light,"[14] the car was a monstrosity that diminished to the point of absurdity the visual impact of the coffin itself, which rested tenuously more than fourteen feet above the ground and had to be tied down with copper wire to avoid its slipping off once the car was pulled into motion by twelve sable horses. (A canopy that crowned the entire apparatus also had to be removed before the car could pass under the Temple Bar archway.)

Spectacle, however, seems capable of playing strange games when it comes to the anticipated results of political affiliation. Carlyle's class-inflected excoriation of the car as a jejune product of Cockneyism, like Greville's imprecation against its vulgarity, is not surprising, for these are the criticisms of aesthetically informed, enlightened conservatives. Thomas Cooper's reaction to the procession and car, however, appears more extraordinary, given this autodidact's long commitment to Chartism. Incarcerated for two years in the early 1840s after being falsely accused of inciting a Hanley crowd to violence, Cooper was best known for his long poetical work, *The Purgatory of Suicides,* written in prison and unconditionally radical in tone. Cooper's decision to watch Wellington's funeral in London, the very city in which the duke had organized massive defenses against Chartist petitioners, is of particular interest; his unabridged admiration for Wellington ("the great pillar of State and most valued counselor of his Queen . . . the most deeply respected and most heartily honoured person in the realm") coalesced with unalloyed gratification at the sight of the procession ("the most impressively grand spectacle I ever beheld").[15] "The varied costume of the English regiments mingled with the kilted High-landers," Cooper wrote in his autobiography,

> and Lancers and Life Guards with the Scotch Greys, rendered the vi-sion picturesque as well as stately. But it was upon the huge funeral car, and the led charger in front of it, that all eyes gazed most wistfully:— above all, it was upon the crimson-velvet covered coffin, *upon* the vast pall—not covered by it, borne aloft, on the car, with the white-plumed cocked hat, and the sword and marshal's baton lying upon the coffin, that all gazed most intently. I watched it—I stretched my neck to get the last sight of the car as it passed along Piccadilly, till it was out of sight; and then I thought the great connecting link of our national life was broken: the great actor in the scenes of the Peninsula and Waterloo—the conqueror of Napoleon—and the chief name in our home political life for many years,—had disappeared.[16]

Cooper's repeated, laudatory references to the prodigious size of the car's various components—the surfeit of bewildering flourishes and details so derided by Carlyle—verifies the claim that for many viewers, spectacle was capable of creating a "coherent representational universe" in which seeming contradictions between competing visual elements were overrid-den by the total effect: "The spectacle exalted the ordinary by means of the extraordinary, the small by means of the large, the real by means of the unreal."[17] In Cooper's case, the symbolic capital expended on the car had not gone to waste. In fact, the car's much excoriated anachronism, registered in complaints about its inaccessibility to interpretation, was al-together lost on Cooper, who instead was recalled by the contraption to his "very childhood . . . passed amid the noise of Wellington's battles."[18] Carlyle's "incoherent huddle" of flags and emblems was for Cooper a fit-ting tribute not only to Wellington but also to Englishness itself: the car's design by committee and its expeditious manufacture had, in this instance, fulfilled one of the prince consort's favorite ideas, "the conception of English arts and crafts as the handmaids of the great achievements of Victorian civilisation."[19]

The conventionality of Cooper's language is as notable as his admiration for the funeral car and procession. He reiterated uncritically the stock phrases and ideological orthodoxies common to the sermons, poems, memoirs, and press reports during the months preceding the funeral. In the popular imagination, Wellington had long been the nation's "pillar of State" and (as has been shown) the queen's "most valued counselor."[20] The *Leeds Mercury*, for example, claimed that Victoria "leaned upon [Wellington] with something like a daughter's veneration."[21] Cooper's "personal" recollection of the funeral, therefore, was filtered through and in large part adjudicated by a language readily available to him in the eulogies. Like Hughes's allusions to the moral example of Wellington in *Tom Brown's School Days*, Cooper's facile co-opting of this language within an autobiographical treatise, a "private" form of writing that ostensibly sought to trace "every thought to the earliest part of one's conscious existence,"[22] illustrated the radically public nature of the duke's legacy and the temporary saturation of a culture by the Wellington literature.

Put simply, Cooper wanted to be "part of it," a desire that nullified political and class antagonisms. Predictably enough, this initial desire combined with an ambition to be identified with a hero corporately hailed as the model of virtuous Englishness. And so Cooper echoed the common estimation of Wellington as "the very personification of English valour and English sagacity. He was an institution in himself. We all felt as if we lived, now *he* was dead, in a different England."[23] Here, Cooper could have been taking a page out of the weekly *Examiner*, which broadcast that "the Duke of Wellington was emphatically English. His patience, his probity, his punctuality in the smallest things, in everything the practical fidelity and reliability of his character, we rejoice to regard as the type of that which has made us the great people that we are."[24]

The funeral, then, could be read typologically by informed spectators as the final chapter in a particular narrative about the English character and its intermittent manifestation in history's great men. All great things, Carlyle had declared in *On Heroes*, have their origins in the thoughts and actions of "the modelers, patterns, . . . the Great Men sent into the world:

the soul of the whole world's history, it may justly be considered, were the history of these."[25] Carlyle's own adverse reaction to Wellington's funeral car in no way diminished the grandiosity of its original conception, which was as a conveyance that would suitably represent the accomplishments of that "emphatically English" hero whose corpse it carried. By necessity, the funeral car contradicted the axioms of simplicity in its summoning of history through an amalgam of symbols.

There was, however, general agreement that the procession itself was "rather a fine sight, and all well done."[26] An anonymous poet in the *Times* extolled the pageant of "marvelous state / Of heralds, soldiers, nobles, foreign Powers, / With baton or with pennon; princes, peers, / Judges, and dignitaries of church and State."[27] The route followed by the cortege had been carefully devised to impress viewers with its symbolical harmony: it had, "for contemporaries, a 'dramatic unity and completeness,' because the procession passed from the wealthy regions of palaces and great mansions, through middle-class areas, to the poorer districts, before finally reaching the metropolitan cathedral."[28] Wellington's body was trundled past various sites with which he had been intimately associated as a statesman and resident of London. The parade mustered on the tiltyard of the Horse Guards, a traditional place of gathering for military reviews on the west side of the Palladian Headquarters of the General Staff. The location had also been the duke's chief place of work as commander in chief. Wellington was known to dismount his horse in front of the building every morning with clocklike regularity, a habit that produced for Londoners a popular image of a frail duke, advanced in years yet dependable to the end. But the assembly of Wellington's funeral procession outside the Horse Guards building proved to be the defining episode in its history as an architectural landmark, the only particular event, for example, mentioned in Ben Weinreb and Christopher Hibbert's prodigious *London Encyclopaedia* under the entry dedicated to the structure.

John Wilson provides a fairly detailed description of the procession, made up of some ten thousand participants:

> The parts of the procession comprised two regiments of the line, a battalion of the royal marines, the household troops, cavalry and infantry,

representatives of every regiment or other corps in the British army, seventeen guns, with their complement of men, a body of Chelsea pensioners, staff officers bearing banners, or escorting the deceased Duke's insignia of office, representations of all the bodies with whom the Duke had stood connected, deputations from public bodies . . . and the persons or the representatives of all the great authorities, including the ministers of state, Prince Albert, and generals or princes from foreign courts.[29]

Wilson neglects to mention the various bands, chaplains, heralds, ushers, pallbearers, paid mourners, and—honoring military tradition—Wellington's charger, with the late duke's boots resting backwards in the stirrups.

The procession was managed, in part, by 5,058 police, who served as parade marshals lining the streets from Chelsea to the City and who ensured that the vast cavalcade moved off at precisely eight o'clock. Indeed, heavily policed social order was decidedly the subject matter of numerous Victorian illustrations commemorating the procession, in the process testifying powerfully to the pacific nature of the British crowd (figure 5.3). The procession made its way along the Mall and up Constitution Hill to Hyde Park Corner. This part of the journey, which formed the westward arm of a vast V pattern, brought the marchers past Buckingham Palace and along the edge of Green Park to Robert Adams's neoclassical masterpiece, Apsley House. Often referred to as "No. 1 London" because "it was the first house to be encountered after passing the toll gates at the top of Knightsbridge, a conspicuous position" in the late eighteenth century,[30] Apsley House could also be said to have accommodated London's "No. 1 citizen," "an impenetrable and omniscient figure, . . . a totem who wore around him the aura and title 'the hero of Waterloo.'"[31] The return of Wellington's corpse to Apsley House momentarily reunited London's most celebrated inhabitant with one of the city's most exclusive pieces of property. From there, the car was turned (lacking a movable axle, this was a difficult operation, and soldiers had to maneuver it by hand) onto Piccadilly, from whence the procession moved south along St. James's Street.

The royal family awaited the passage of the cortege on a balcony in St. James's Palace. Here, just as the parade turned east into Pall Mall, the

FIGURE 5.3 *The Strand—The Procession Passing St. Clement's, Illustrated London News*, 27 November 1852.

final act in that drama commemorated by Winterhalter's painting was played out. With sentimental virtuosity, a writer for the *Illustrated London News* located the procession's emotional crescendo at the moment the car passed the royal audience: "Mournfully, amid the tears of the spectators in the balconies, the gorgeous and towering car approached St. James's Palace. In a few minutes the stately dais, with the sacred remains of the Queen's fastest friend—her greatest but most loyal subject—slowly passed before the gaze of the Sovereign and the Royal children. We shall not intrude upon the grief of the illustrious circle."[32] Trailing off deferentially, the passage centralized the car as the physical and visceral nucleus of the cortege. It also reinforced a relationship of benign condescension between the hero and a female sovereign still somewhat unseasoned in the subtleties of royal governance. Wellington's paternal advice would be much missed—or so the writer assumed in this maudlin interpretation of the profound "grief of the illustrious circle."[33] The queen shed tears, it was intimated, at the sight of the ducal car; its sublime presence induced royal catharsis. But the writer absented himself from the intimacy of the royal circle in a linguistic gesture of profound respect.

Such discretion was exceptional in the general coverage. A *Times* correspondent's glowing report on the day of the funeral provided a fitting commentary on the public enthusiasm that lent a festive mood to the parade, an almost carnival-like atmosphere that prevailed in spite of the dampness and cold of a fall day: "It is impossible to convey any idea of the excitement which prevailed yesterday throughout the metropolis with reference to the ceremonial which takes place today. On no public occasion has anything at all approaching it ever been manifested. The streets have been blocked up with conveyances to an unprecedented extent, and the pavements so crowded with foot passengers that it was with the greatest difficulty people could get from point to point."[34]

If the *Times's* prefuneral exuberance was somewhat premature, it was not contradicted by the unfolding of the procession, which lasted just over four hours and safely deposited the duke's body at St. Paul's at precisely 12:10 in the afternoon. The *Morning Herald* concluded that the day of the funeral had been "emphatically and incomparably the greatest public day for people of every age, class, and character that has ever been known in London."[35] The final kilometers of the car's pilgrimage involved its passing through Trafalgar Square via Cockspur Street, into the Strand, under Temple Bar onto Fleet Street, and finally up Ludgate Hill to reach the west entrance of the cathedral. Most of the specially invited mourners gathered there had been waiting in the frigid interior for some time, "thrown upon their own resources for some means of passing the long hours until the arrival of the funeral cortège" and packed into makeshift seating tiers.[36] They stared into a gloom insufficiently illuminated by gas jets repeatedly extinguished by gusts of frigid air and could only make their escape after 3:00, when all the parish churches in England tolled their bells and the duke's coffin was lowered into the vault to the tune of the "Dead March in Saul." At the funeral's climax, the cathedral service was something of a fiasco, even if it saw "all the scattered elements of the procession . . . condensed into a gorgeous mass" under St. Paul's dome.[37]

That acute condensation was itself to blame for a ceremony numerous papers considered a travesty. The great church may have been filled with "thousands of the fairest, the bravest, the highest, the noblest in the land," but the gravity of the assemblage was compromised by choristers who took books of service and "flung them up in handsful," as a result of which "a general scramble took place . . . those on the lower benches who were supplied making pellets of the remainder, and casting them at the occupants of the back benches."[38] "The moral atmosphere in St. Paul's was far less solemn than we had expected it to be," noted the *Age;* "the majority of spectators had attained their seats only after such struggling as was common a few days ago round Chelsea Hospital . . . and the loud hum of careless conversation which resounded through the building, and the general wearing of hats in the naves . . . were by no means symptomatic of a profoundly impressed body of spectators."[39]

The disappointment registered in these accounts suggests that the burial ceremony was fundamentally discordant with the good order that characterized the explicitly secular procession preceding it. Prime Minister Derby was able to exult in a job well done in a speech to the House of Lords shortly after the funeral:

> But it would be most unjust if I were to withhold . . . the tribute of your admiration and satisfaction at the perfect organization, the admirable arrangements, the entire discipline with which the whole of that great ceremony was marshaled and conducted, and at the discretion and the judgment which were manifested by all those civil and military authorities who took a part in carrying it out. . . . My lords, I [further] allude to that upon which we may look with pride and gratification—I mean the admirable temper, patience, forbearance, and good conduct which was manifested by the whole of these incredible masses.[40]

Derby's praise categorically and officially consecrated the funeral as a triumphant event, but it was at odds with those other accounts of the cathedral ceremony just quoted, less indiscriminate versions that touched upon an incongruity that, in turn, hinted at the problems entailed in celebrating the life and death of a Victorian soldier-hero through the recollection of pagan ritual. Buried in the cathedral-church of Protestant England in a service led by the dean of St. Paul's, Wellington's body in the procession had been presided over by the Lord Chamberlain's Office, a nonclerical bureau responsible to the College of Arms.[41] The apparent incompatibility of pageant with interment found its tangential expression in a perceived antithesis between "the barbarism of the recent show" and the authentic, Christian "sentiment that lay beneath it."[42]

This observation returns us to a discussion about exhibitions and spectacles, for in complaining about the "mismanagement of every detail connected with the public accommodation left to the charge of the cathedral authorities," critics were identifying an inappropriate invasion of the godless procession into a holy place, where much the same could be said of public behavior as of the parade itself: "It was to be a show, unequaled for magnificence, and so forth; and as the public was invited to a show, to a show it went."[43] Among the immediate and most ubiquitous responses to this "show" were those that sought to seamlessly incorporate Wellington into a commemorative practice that erased any hints of ignominy. Anglican ministers, in particular, tended to err on the side of caution when it came to the duke's faith, compensating for their necessary ignorance about the hero's Christian beliefs by emphasizing his divinely sanctioned role as a "mighty instrument of blessing." Various ecclesiastical writers wrestled with the primary contradiction between parochial ceremony and mundane show, attempting a reconciliation by displacing the terms of debate onto the perplexing question of Wellington's own religious commitments. Wellington was represented not only as a pillar of state but also as a defender of the Christian faith, and thus, his function as ideal exemplar could be conserved.

Marie Maurice, whose biography was intended to contribute to the proper moral and religious training of "the children of England," made Wellington's name into a paradigm for Christian instruction: "To one so perfectly truthful, and upright, anything like an empty profession would be revolting, and therefore more heartily do we welcome proofs which we possess, that the God who had kept him all his life long, who had raised him up as a mighty instrument of blessing, was more and more honoured and served by him as he drew nearer to the close of life."[44] At the same time, an assertion of the duke's religious conviction resolved apprehensions about the profane revelry through insistence on its temporal appropriateness for a man whose earthly work appeared to be guided by celestial powers. The procession, like so many of the religious discourses delivered in the weeks preceding it, was an occasion to "draw the attention of men's thoughts, from the dazzling achievements of the Duke's wonderful life, up to the God who wrought such wonders for us."[45] John Baines argued in a commemorative sermon that the Bible provided numerous examples of the burial of Christian kings and princes. The Gospel thus countenanced through precedent the resplendent affair that was Wellington's funeral: "Here then we have the recognition and the approval of honouring to the utmost of our power the mighty dead, and investing the last offices we can pay them, with all the grandeur, solemnity, and magnificence we can."[46] John Manly abbreviated a sentiment common to various Church of England clerics who took up the subject of Wellington, noting that even if the pulpit was "not the place for political harangue, for worldly eulogy, for mere critical acumen or intellectual display," ministers might still "seize upon secular events to suggest spiritual lessons, or make the death of the mighty an occasion of moral instruction to the living."[47]

This last justification intimates a truth wholly uncongenial to Maurice's school of inculpable, Christian biography, which never reveals the precise nature of those "proofs" of the duke's godliness: Wellington's religious observances were by no means conscientious, just as his adherence to church doctrine or his Christian beliefs could never be ascertained beyond the level of conjecture. According to John Wilson, "How much [Wellington] was affected at any time by the most powerful of all agencies upon human character—the only agency which can render it truly good at the core, the agency of revealed truth as correctly understood from the sacred scriptures—there is little direct evidence to show."[48] Neither Maxwell nor Longford made any mention of Wellington's religiosity, dignifying instead the resolutely secular soldier-hero whose image agreed better with eighteenth- and early nineteenth-century Hanoverian mores than with the evangelical codes of religious and moral conduct that came to prevail in the early Victorian era.

Even more telling are the remarkable series of letters that constitute the uneasy correspondence of Wellington with "Miss J." between 1834 and 1851. Only twenty years old at the time this correspondence began,

Miss A. M. Jenkyns was an impulsive and enthusiastic writer, extraordinarily anxious for the conversion of those around her. After his second visit to Jenkins, on which occasion Wellington rashly declared his love for the beautiful young woman, she expressed her extreme indignation in a letter of 12 January 1835: "I should not be surprised (although rest assured, I do not desire it) at any vengeance God saw fit to shower down for such a dreadful intention upon Your Grace's head. Oh may His Holy Spirit convince you of the heinousness of the sin in question, leading you from darkness to light."[49] Jenkyns's evident disgust did not prevent her from regularly pestering Wellington with proselytizing missives, and in her diary for 1 October 1835, she was hopeful of the great man's change of heart: "Perhaps the Duke's conversion is at hand! Lord if this be the case permit me through Thy Power and Grace to become the source of deep spiritual consolation to his soul."[50] Wellington, however, resisted the confessional mode throughout the period of his association with Jenkyns, at one point tersely responding to her religious ecstasies with the statement that "I am not capable, I am sorry to acknowledge, on entering on a discussion on the topics in your letter."[51] He later noted conclusively his lack of interest in doctrinal or spiritual discussions: "The Duke is unfortunately for him not sufficiently informed to enable Him to write upon some of the Higher and more sacred Topicks of Miss J.'s letters."[52] When she received news of Wellington's death, Jenkyns could only lament the state of an unrepentant soul.

As Graham Dawson has shown, the "emergence of [a] qualitatively new kind of soldier hero"—the "Christian soldier" embodied most conspicuously in Sir Henry Havelock, who helped suppress the Indian Rebellion —was a fact of the mid- to late 1850s, a consequence of new hagiographic impulses that postdated Wellington, whose own reputation as a great military captain never lost its association with a distinctly carnal, "brutal and licentious soldiery."[53] The few clergymen who felt obliged to gauge the authenticity of the duke's faith found themselves immersed in speculation. After recalling the "mournful pageants of the last week . . . on which were lavished the wealth and the art of the widest and richest of earthly empires," J. De Kewer Williams commented, "Of his [Wellington's] soul, which is the Lord's as much as any other man's, we have nothing to say, being mindful of the reproof, 'Who art thou that judgest another man's servant? To his own master he standeth or falleth.'"[54] What Williams *did* know was that Wellington "attended the early service at the Chapel Royal at St. James's . . . and that the Bible found in his bookcase seems to have been well read."[55] It seems fairly clear that the "knowable" here is as nebulous as the emotional states of the royal family in the *ILN* passage quoted earlier, when the funeral car passed St. James's Palace.

Wellington himself viewed religious observance as a duty or trust required of a public man and servant of the Crown. There is no tone of evangelical fervor in a letter he wrote to Angela Burdett-Coutts on 11 September 1849: "I consider that the attendance at Divine Service in Publick is a Duty upon every individual in High Station, who has a large House and Many Servants, and whose example might influence the Conduct of others."[56] In such a statement, Wellington explicitly acknowledges and submits to the public's double expectation of him. His social position and unique reputation demand exemplary behavior with regard to social and religious form. Wellington perceives himself as one of Carlyle's "modelers," as a "Great Man sent into the world."

Wellington's funeral, then, marked a late transition point between the comparative hedonism of early nineteenth-century state obsequies (one thinks in particular of Nelson, whose epicurean life and dramatic death were celebrated most conspicuously in the ephemeral forms of the broadside ballad, the chapbook, the romantic history, and the biography) and a later "convergence of the national military pantheon with the Christian soldier tradition."[57] The curious integration of secular hero worship with religious edification in Wellington funeral sermons therefore produced a generic hybrid bridging past and present, an annexation to which the Church of England, a place of Christian worship but also a national institution, was well adapted. In John Wolffe's words, "Preachers had an opportunity to project through the image of the deceased those qualities that they themselves perceived as most fundamental to national life. . . . The Duke of Wellington was portrayed as the pre-eminent hero, the supreme protector of the nation, and God's agent in overcoming bondage and idolatry from India to Spain, and raising England to new heights of national eminence."[58]

John Hayden's sermon in Trinity Chapel, High Wycombe, in late November 1852 was a striking example of how the fame of a military hero apparently uninterested in matters of the soul could be arrogated to religious discourse without fostering any serious predicaments. Hayden's oration was conspicuous, in fact, for its nonecclesiastical content and tone. It evaluated the duke's character under the same four subheadings the *Times* had used (Wellington's greatness as a commander, ambassador, statesman, and patriot) and focused on the hero's worldly accomplishments: Wellington's "loyalty was unimpeachable, and his zeal for his country's safety and prosperity of such a nature, that . . . no difficulties or dangers could extinguish." The lesson to be taken away from Hayden's address had little to do with salvation or the afterlife; rather, his congregation was urged to "cherish . . . as the departed Duke always cherished, a profound sense of loyalty and love to your country." As for the question of Wellington's personal credo, Hayden made no excuses for his ignorance: "If I have said nothing respecting him on the subject of religion, it is because I am ignorant of the views and feelings he entertained on that which, above all other subjects, is of infinite and everlasting importance."[59]

Clearly, this ignorance in no way circumscribed Hayden's ability to make Wellington into an appropriate exemplar for a Christian audience. Evidently, the church was as deeply invested in creating a public image of the duke as the nation's defender as were the organizers of the Great Exhibition, that exclusively secular congregation of commodity worshipers. It could be argued that, for many clergy in the Anglican church, patriotism was a subject similar to religion in its "infinite and everlasting" importance. Nationalist sentiment was enunciated with a fervor that Wellington's own religious ambivalence denied to those who would turn him into a saintly figure. And so Wellington's private merits—patience, loyalty, common sense, and so on—were publicized in such a way that they were figuratively aligned with Christian virtues. Wellington was reconstructed within the venue of the church as every Christian soldier's guide, as a great commander in the fight for the kingdom of heaven; the language of encouragement in this prolonged spiritual battle was, understandably, secular, borrowed from the epic vernacular of military adventures. "How great was this man!" A. M. Close exclaimed near the end of his memorial sermon at Cheltenham, "How deservedly honoured by his countrymen! How justly due to him these gorgeous national obsequies!"[60] This deification of immaculate humanity from the pulpit of the national church propitiated any sense that an intrusion of secular homage into the realm of the sacred was inappropriate.

I am not trying to argue that the church was consciously and rather disingenuously engaged in a project that would see an unsuitably secular subject—the Wellington, for example, of Patrick Delaforce's book, a lifelong beau who "could and did flirt with attractive married ladies"[61]—reclaimed and expurgated for religious use. Rather, two discursive traditions, the military and the religious, were enthusiastically coupled in many of the funeral sermons. Given that both traditions were fundamentally typological, portraying Wellington as a salvation figure, it could be argued that a third ideological category, that of national exemplarity, superseded and thereby canceled any serious contradiction. Wellington's popular reputation at midcentury as the most laudable of English soldiers, diplomats, and politicians—as, effectively, the antitype of male Englishness—served to bind together, however contingently, church and state in a way that was useful to members of the Anglican establishment, whose institutional identity since the time of Henry VIII had never really depended on any such radical distinctions. The duke's sexual foibles and past defamation were not so much eschewed in his canonization/anglicization (every soldier has his vices, every statesman his falls from grace) as they were wholly irrelevant and hence invisible to those who would annex the Wellington legend to a story about righteous destiny, militant Christianity, and a deity who clearly favored the British in their war against Napoleonic France.

Wellington achieved his own supreme apotheosis when his military victories were read, within the typological framework of promise and fulfillment, as instances of divine emancipation. Wellington became Christlike, a tool of God's righteous vengeance, and hence a Christian soldier in spite of his apparent indifference to spiritual matters: "Shall we refuse to do homage to his memory because he drew the sword? Did he not save more lives than he destroyed?—and did he ever destroy, but to save?"[62] To mourn and esteem Wellington was not only to honor the nation, it was to worship God, a second instance of triple veneration that complemented the secular nativity scene of Winterhalter's *The First of May*. John Scott's memorial sermon at Holy Trinity Church before the mayor and city corporation of Hull offered what is perhaps the most explicit example of this consolidation. "It is our business as ministers of Christ," Scott noted at the beginning of his exhortation, "to seek rather to rouse and benefit the living than to eulogize the dead: but surely I may be forgiven, if, on an occasion like the present, I seek to excite your gratitude to the Giver of all good, by briefly recalling your attention to the mighty benefits and blessings bestowed upon this nation . . . by the hand which now moulders in the grave."[63] Here, the English were figured as a chosen people, a nineteenth-century analogue to the Old Testament Israelites. Wellington was "bestowed" on the nation in much the same way as the biblical judges and kings were directly entrusted by God to guide his people according to his divine will and precepts.

This particular return to a distant past, like the Caesarism of the special *Illustrated London News* masthead in figure 0.1, illustrated that death is what Elisabeth Bronfen calls a "privileged trope," a term that "grounds the way a culture stabilises and represents itself, yet does so as a signifier with an incessantly receding, ungraspable signified which invariably always points self-reflexively to other signifiers."[64] For Church of England clergy, Wellington's death was manifestly an occasion for the expression of sorrow through communal mourning and an opportunity to remind parishioners of the "ungraspable," their own mortality: "Brethren, let me ask, are you prepared to die?" But Wellington's death also "grounded" British culture in 1852 by offering a prime opportunity to reminisce about national superiority, a repeatedly importuned theme whose commonplace assertion was that "Britain was honoured as the instrument in beating back and crushing the tyrant [Napoleon]—in delivering the nations of Europe from his grasp—in letting the oppressed go free."[65]

The groundwork for Wellington's assumption of this uniquely elevated position in ecclesiastical discourse had, of course, already been laid. The most immediate and arguably most influential precedent for Wellington's characterization as the national savior was to be found in the national press, which engaged in a contest of compromise with the hero's past in order to absolve him of terrestrial profligacies. The *Chronicle*, for example, was able to compliment those journals whose commemorations were "written with a large, strong, deep, and true appreciation of the Duke's character," a tribute to "proper" journalism congruent with its own decorous appreciation. The paper concluded, however, by noting that "almost the only exceptions to the universal voice of the United Kingdom were certain rabid attacks which the organs of the Ultramontane faction in Ireland directed against the memory of the most illustrious of Irishmen."[66] Chapter 6 examines the conflict between Irish and English presses in order to consider, once again, who represented the dead hero and how his representation disclosed the interests of the proxies who laid claim to or disassociated themselves from him.

SIX

Irish Opposition

THE WAR of words that took place between the English and Irish presses during the sixty-five days that Wellington's body awaited burial was not so much an anomalous contest engendered by the unique circumstance of the duke's death as it was a subplot in a continuing struggle between margin and center that received a pronounced charge from this circumstance and long outlived it. In this sense, the "resolution" that was Wellington's death ceremony—its function as a "collective expression of a culture's imagination"[1]—encouraged a working through of national conflict in language rather than in actuality, however unbalanced and ineffective that process proved to be. A better understanding of this process requires a brief step back in history to consider Wellington's own attitudes toward the country of his birth.

In the spring of 1809, Arthur Wellesley (he did not become the Duke of Wellington until 1814) made what was to be his final visit to Ireland. He had temporarily removed himself from London the previous October to return to Ireland, a decision taken on the advice of the Duke of Richmond, who thought it best that Wellesley lie low while waiting to defend himself at the military inquiry into the Convention of Cintra. The inquiry itself, an infamous "morass of intrigue into which he . . . slithered" quite involuntarily,[2] brought General Wellesley back to England from a four-month stint in Portugal, where he had forced the retreat of General Henri François, Count of Laborde's forces at Roliça and led a decisive victory against General Androche Junot's army at Vimeiro. On 4 April 1809, Wellesley resigned as chief secretary for Ireland, a post he had held along with that of privy councillor since 1807. This move marked the end of sixteen years of service for the parliaments of both Ireland (as member for the borough of Trim) and England (as member, in turn, for Rye, Midsall, Newport, and Tralee). It also marked the peremptory end of his life in Ireland. Ten days after his resignation, Wellesley was sailing toward Portugal aboard the *Surveillante*. On 12 May, he and his troops crossed the Douro River to liberate Oporto from the French invaders, and over the course of the next five years, he would achieve lasting renown as victor at the Battles of Ciudad Rodrigo, Badajoz, Salamanca, Vitoria, San Sebastian, Nivelle, and Toulouse. After Napoleon's abdication in 1814, he would make his first return to Britain since his departure on the *Surveillante*, to "live among us," as one poet put it, "as a part / Of hearth and home,"[3] taking a seat in the British House of Lords on 28 June as field marshal, the First Duke of Wellington.

Wellington's apparently conscious decision to avoid Ireland after the age of forty came to be interpreted by his Irish detractors as a vindictive disinheritance. Long-suffering Ireland was abandoned in favor of a whole-hearted and parsimonious adoption of all things English. "The Duke did not serve his native country," claimed the *Galway Vindicator*, "he served a foreign nation and he had all the attributes of a hireling or mercenary commander."[4] A more generous assessment, however, would suggest that Wellington, readily anglicized by the English as one of their own on his return from the peninsular campaigns, put forever behind him any questions about rank and status that might be associated with the Anglo-Irish peerage into which he was born at Mornington House, Dublin. That "unpretending edifice" was eventually to be celebrated as "the spot where Erin presented to Britain a hero who was destined eventually to overrule the aspirings of him whom Corsica's more sunny isle was just then about to bring forth."[5] With his Englishness permanently affirmed on his return to "hearth and home" in 1814—to "us," as the poet quoted earlier put it—Wellington's own, necessarily equivocal relationship with Ireland could be laid to rest. He had returned to the country from which, according to popular legend, his family departed in the late twelfth century, when a certain Wellesley of Somerset, serving as standard bearer for Henry II, accompanied the king on his invasion of Ireland.[6]

John Bull proclaimed Wellington's Anglo purity in its reiteration of this account: "Arthur Wellesley . . . was descended from an ancient Saxon family which took its name from the manor of Wellesleigh, in Somersetshire, and a branch of which settled, as far back as the reign of Henry II, in Ireland."[7] Intermarrying within the privileged circle of Anglo-Norman families of the pale among whom they lived, the Wellesleys (after the time of Charles I, the Wesleys) experienced a "strikingly homogeneous past" for six centuries. Behind Arthur "stretched an embattled English race who had occupied an alien land, marrying strictly with their own kind and becoming not only a ruling caste but a ruling garrison." If he expressed no remorse for having escaped Ireland, "it would be hard for Wellington to escape from such a heredity."[8]

Indeed, the duke's inability to escape the bred-in-the-bone garrison mentality of the Anglo-Irish peerage became a generally recognized fact, a defining feature of his "Englishness" even in those tentative posthumous tributes that insisted on calling him an Irishman while recognizing that his interests were fundamentally inimical to the popular, reformist nationalism represented by his political rival, Daniel O'Connell, founder of the Catholic Association. A writer in the *Belfast Mercury* of 18 September 1852 noted, "The English are gratified to discover in the Duke those characteristics which they believe distinguish themselves. Though they must admit he was an Irishman by birth, yet, as his family on both sides, is originally English, we cannot complain of them for speaking of him as one of themselves; and this more especially when his characteristics as well as his leanings were strongly English." The writer closed, however, "with a word of regret, that this illustrious and glorious Irishman did not turn the resources of his authority and his mind more to the condition of his native land. . . . It would have added a ray of mild splendour to the brighter effulgence of his name, if he had tried to conquer our miseries and our social evils."[9] In the rather subtle distinction drawn between Wellington's "characteristic" Englishness and his "native" Irishness—a distinction between his upbringing as a member of a socially and culturally insulated aristocracy, on the one hand, and the mundane fact of his birth in Ireland, on the other—resides the locus of the ideological struggle that took place in the English and Irish presses immediately after his death.

This struggle was instigated by the *Galway Vindicator* but was intensified, somewhat surprisingly, by the *Times,* whose eloquent Wellington tribute of 15 September opened with lines that were to be quoted repeatedly by other newspapers as the final statement on the hero's distinction: "The Duke of Wellington had exhausted nature and exhausted glory. His career was one unclouded longest day, filled from dawn to nightfall with renowned actions, animated by unfailing energy in the public service, guided by unswerving principles of conduct and of statesmanship."[10] The *Times*'s meticulous and articulate Wellington biography in this and subsequent numbers contributed to its peerless reputation as (to quote the *Belfast Mercury*) a "great organ, whose utterances are those of millions."[11] "What has been done by the *Times* may be referred to as affording no inapt illustration of the state of public feeling," the *Mercury* continued; "its fine historic and philosophic memoir of the illustrious dead occupied over thirty columns; and for four successive days, its chief article each day has been devoted to the same theme."[12] As a periodical of high repute whose "Life of Wellington" was heavily cited in other posthumous tributes, the *Times* was burdened with a considerable responsibility to be consistently discriminating and tactful in its coverage. But its decision to wade into the dispute about Wellington's national identity by lambasting the "wreath, not of bays, but of prickly holly"[13] laid upon the duke by certain members of the Irish press ultimately led to its denunciation by several Irish contemporaries as a propagator of "insolent clamours" and "swaggering and inflated essays."[14]

On 21 September, the *Times* published a number of responses to Wellington's death culled from Irish and French newspapers. A lengthy quotation from the *Galway Vindicator* of 18 September, which included that paper's inflammatory assessment of the duke as an example of "stolid, stupid, swinish Englishmen" who had "tarnished the brilliancy of his fame by subjecting himself to the censure of history,"[15] was supplemented with another editorial in an ongoing series about the "religious equality movement"—a catchall phrase coined by the *Times* to designate any brand of pro-Catholic advocacy that sought to end special Protestant entitlements in Ireland. Throughout the autumn of 1852, the *Times* had linked the "movement" with a corrupt priesthood, stressing repeatedly that Irish laypeople were the dupes of "the fractious and violent conduct of the Roman Catholic priests."[16] Assuming the mantle of Protestant Britain's defender, the *Times* declared that the "time has gone by when this country could be startled or moved by threats of Irish rebellion or disaffection, however loudly bellowed forth, and however frequently reiterated."[17] It confidently identified the primary source of such disaffection: "The Roman Catholic priesthood are ruining and desolating Ireland fast enough, without [our] handing over to them the property of the Establishment to assist them in their odious and unholy work."[18]

The *Times*, then, ensured that its homage to Wellington after 14 September coincided with a relentless heckling of the Irish Catholic hierarchy and its supporters in the periodical press. The *Belfast Mercury* expressed its dismay with the *Times* in an issue for early October, asking, "Is it right and proper—is it becoming—is it in conformity with humane feeling—that [the *Times*] . . . should assail us with attacks and sneers that are felt and resented more or less by the mass of the Irish nation?"[19] The daily *Freeman's Journal* of Dublin was less circumspect in its disapproval, alluding vaguely to a long-term project on the part of the *Times* to establish its reputation as the voice of England—of Saxondom—through the defamation of the Celt. "Not content with alleging the utter prostration of the Celtic Irishman, his degeneracy, his hopelessly irreclaimable savagery," the article stated, "the *Times* has long set up the claim of the Anglo-Saxon to be the perfection of humanity—the true *Anax Andron*." The qualities of "your true Anglo-Saxon" were derided in turn: he "carries his humbug about with him like a vapour, of convex-lenslike properties, seen through which his points loom large, and he walks the earth like a very giant, compared with whom even Titan was only a size above Tom Thumb."[20]

This implicit attack on Wellington, mid-nineteenth-century Britain's most widely recognized model of imperious masculinity, embraced the mythology of Celticism. Such linguistic reversion, which constructed "a continuous, unaltered [Celtic] tradition, stretching back to remote antiquity,"[21] lent to the paper a dignity that circumstances would otherwise have contradicted. Prys Morgan's comments on language and nationalism help to explain this and other instances in which newspapers arguing for the primacy of English or Irish blood in Wellington fell back upon allusions to the duke's Saxon or Celtic lineage: "The Celts in fact had never been associated with the British Isles, but that did not really matter, for they were a magnificent race of conquerors who had thundered across Europe in their chariots. . . . The Celts reflected the fantasies of the age, and in [Ireland] they provided the constricted . . . nation, which had little to commend it in its present state, with an unimaginably grandiose past, by way of consolation."[22] Any consolation, however, was far from sufficient. The *Freeman's Journal* felt obliged to continue its assaults against the English in subsequent, increasingly vituperative columns.

The inherent contradictions of such appeals to pure racial inheritance, however, became more visible as the *Freeman's Journal* strove to position itself as both the defender of Celtic honor and the prosecutor of English arrogance. In the process, it lost sight of its earlier, rhetorically incumbent drive to tag Wellington as "your true Anglo-Saxon," and it gradually reclaimed the hero as one of Ireland's wayward sons. In short, the *Journal* wanted to play two games at once as it remonstrated with the *Times.* It wanted to cast Wellington as simply one more autocrat in a long line of political oppressors, but it also wanted to deny the English any prerogative over his undeniably distinguished achievements on the battlefield. In an interpretation of the duke's early career that was intended to exacerbate the indignation of its English rivals on the day of the funeral, the *Journal* showed itself capable of making an abrupt argumentative turnaround:

> Young Wellesley carried to his first field in India nothing English, but his commission. The qualities that determined Assaye and captured Seringapatam were not English, for they were not acquired in

England by education or training. . . . England should be chastened by the reflection that she honours today with more than regal honours one of that race which she has scourged, and chained, and proscribed for ages . . . that an Irishman established that peace out which [*sic*] have sprung her commercial grandeur—her colonization—her most cherished institutions—in fact, all that constitutes the wonderful aggregate which men call "England."[23]

In this striking revision, the *Freeman's Journal* gestured toward a narrative binary that, in large part, regulated the ways in which members of the oppositional press could represent the dead Wellington. Two rhetorical strategies were available to those Irish periodicals that resisted the entreaty to "mourn / For him whose dust in pomp is borne / Along the deep-thronged way."[24] And evidently, both could be exploited by the same newspaper at different moments. First, they could consent to the hero's essential Englishness, wholly ceding Wellington to the English in order to reproach him vicariously through the reviling of English idiosyncrasies and prejudices. Thus, the *Journal* charged, "it is notorious that the Duke had become so identified in all things with England . . . that his chief, if not his only irremediable mortification, was that he was born in Ireland and of Irish parents. While living, he despised the race from which he sprang; and . . . a just sense of self-respect will keep this people from worshiping at his tomb."[25] Second, they could stubbornly maintain the ascendancy of birthplace, insisting on Wellington's Irishness in an ideological tug-of-war emphasizing identity and possession: "The Irishman, Wellington, has gone after the Englishman Peel—the two eyes of England are out. Henceforth she will want—but we trust will not obtain—Irishmen to guide her armies, and councils, she will be obliged to trust to her sons who are destitute alike of the eloquence of Burke and the courage of Wellington."[26] Again and again, Irish newspapers reverted to one or the other of these strategic alternatives as they confronted the pervasive image of Wellington as an exclusive possession of the English, not only as "the foremost man of England . . . [and] the purest and the truest patriot of our land"[27] but also as the hero who had discharged the last shot in "the holy cause of our holy faith" at Waterloo, leading the "victory over fallen

Romanism" and hence earning the title of "our Protestant Champion Wellington!"[28]

To suggest that Irish newspapers were constrained to adopt one of two competing rhetorical modes is not to say that they were inherently vulnerable to a defect in representation—that they were unable to evacuate a self-constructed binary system that bedeviled them with contradictions. Rather, this either/or-ism might be called the necessary polemical form taken in any altercation over the essential features of Irishness or Englishness mediated through a figure that could be a legitimate delegate for either "identity." Most notably, the contradiction inherent in the simultaneous promotion of Wellington as an exemplary Englishman and Irishman is further evidence of the hero's posthumous constitution in discourse. If, as Graham Dawson has argued, the existence of such contradictions serves as an opportunity to witness the construction of "the soldier hero as a form of imagined masculinity,"[29] it also encourages us to see such heroes as ideological sites in which imagined nationalities are tested and contested.

The language used in this particular confrontation became increasingly convoluted and retributive, even as it kept slipping credulously into the Celt/Saxon distinction. In part, the debate itself must be understood as an effect of the Irish potato famine, a catastrophe that occurred toward the end of Wellington's life and served as a catalyst for both Celtic revival in Ireland and escalated paranoia about Irish defilement in England. "Ireland after the famines of the mid-nineteenth century was a sort of nowhere," Declan Kiberd has written, "waiting for its appropriate images and symbols to be inscribed in it."[30] Wellington's death was manipulated by antagonists in the debate about Irish and English identity to turn him into one of these symbols.

According to some estimates, the famine truly ended only in the year of Wellington's death, at a cost of 1.2 million lives and the eventual emigration of nearly 2 million.[31] The Great Hunger, along with the subsequent influx of destitute Irish into centers such as Liverpool, Bristol, and London and the ensuing moral panic that seemed "to confirm British stereotypes of Irish degradation,"[32] reinvigorated contentious debates about Irishness and consequently made an indelible contribution to the tenacious "image of

Ireland as not-England."[33] Even if it remained a largely implicit subtext in a controversy whose complexities and occasional contradictions tended to obscure the relative simplicity of what was ultimately at stake—was Wellington one of us or one of them?—the famine inaugurated in England a period of increased hostility toward the Irish that was fostered by and epitomized in the stereotype of the disheveled, quarrelsome, and inebriated Irish peasant, occasionally a picturesque and always an antediluvian figure. The famine, then, was a persistent influence in the Anglo-Irish battle over Wellington's identity. The unrestrained, anti-Wellington hyperbole of the *Galway Vindicator* and *Freeman's Journal,* challenged reflexively through the disparaging satire of the *Age* and *Morning Herald,* created an atmosphere in which already entrenched, postfamine, normally "implicit primitivist assumptions" about the Irish became increasingly conspicuous as the English press persisted in making "observations on the state of the Irish."[34]

In turn, recollections of Wellington's own complacent response to the famine in his final year as a member of Peel's administration contributed to the ambivalence and hostility with which various members of the Irish press treated him after his death. As P. Gray has observed, "Wellington relied heavily for information [about the effects of the famine] on his Irish Tory correspondents ... [choosing] to believe the assertions from his gentry correspondents that the 'potato panick' and its social consequences had been exaggerated."[35] Could the essentializing rhetoric of otherness constructed in the imperative of mutual exclusion that made of Wellington "one of us" or "one of them" be sustained, given that the Anglo-Irish peer's affiliations were inevitably ambivalent and hence controversial?

Such questions emerge from the problems inherent in defining national identity itself, problems that were compounded in Wellington's case by his final departure from Ireland to eventually become England's instrument of freedom and the embodiment of English national spirit. "When did any nation wisely determine for order and freedom without enlisting at once the sympathies of England?" queried a lecturer at the Young Men's Reading Society in 1853; "England determines to aid—and never did she possess, by the blessing of God, a subject and a soldier better calculated to carry out her intentions than General Sir Arthur Wellesley."[36] Here, once again, individual gallantry coincides unproblematically with national destiny. Wellington typifies Englishness itself by carrying out the will of the English, with and to whom he indisputably belongs.

As I have already argued, however, Englishness is not a fixed identity. Rather, it is a site of contestation, "a terrain of struggle," in Catherine Hall's words, "as to what it means to be English."[37] Englishness therefore engenders its own historically contingent but highly portentous rules for exclusion and inclusion: those who "belong" are determined, in large measure, through a process of elimination, through the disqualification of the non- or un-English. Similarly, it follows that "Irishness [is] a category . . . always in transition, under construction, and in tension with other definitions."[38] National identity and internal unity can only be established, and this always precariously, with constant reference to alien nations and peoples.

In the case of the expatriate Wellington, the opposing yet interdependent natures of Irishness and Englishness, their status as contested and contingent categories, were especially pronounced. As one scholar has pointed out, the seeds of this contest were evident in Wellington's own equivocal relationship to Ireland, in the "internal tensions in Wellington's attitude towards Ireland and Irish policy":

> It might be helpful . . . to envisage two Wellingtons. The first, and more familiar, is that of Wellington the Great Briton; the Olympian defender of the national interest, the loyal minister and advisor of the sovereign, the embodiment of patriotic duty. This is Wellington the pragmatic conservative, the ally of Robert Peel, the skillful manager of intractable Tory peers in the House of Lords, the Red Tapist. . . . There was [however] . . . another Wellington—the man who was born, apprenticed and married into the Anglo-Irish gentry, and whose attitudes and preoccupations revealed at least the residual marks of that connection. This was a Wellington obsessive in his defence of concrete Protestant religious and temporal interests—of Protestant ascendancy —in Ireland; a man whose latent passions revealed him to possess something more than a "British" concern for established property rights and civil order in the "sister land."[39]

Wellington, in other words, can be legitimately positioned as both the *Freeman's Journal*'s "great warrior" who had "forsaken and despised his fatherland"[40] and as the *Times*'s "type and model of an Englishman."[41] His own ambivalent relation to Ireland enabled these seemingly contradictory responses.

Wellington's apparent disdain for Ireland was manifested in such petty acts as the inclusion in his 1808 will of a codicil directing that his son, Arthur Richard, "and any child I may have as a consequence of the existing pregnancy of my wife, may not be allowed to live in Ireland or even to go there or to have any connection with that country."[42] He was also doggedly opposed to the Catholic Association, his truculence on this issue confirmed in speeches before the House of Lords in which the duke, whose chief "concern was to uphold the intermeshing elements of . . . Protestant ascendancy, the established 'Church of England in Ireland,'"[43] argued for the use of force to suppress any Catholic insurrection and other "outrages . . . by prohibiting people from leaving their homes from sunset to sunrise, and by punishing them if they be found absent from their homes."[44] Yet by the time he introduced the Roman Catholic Relief Bill in 1829, Wellington could be perceived as a man whose personal distaste for the land of his birth was consistently tempered by a sincere desire to do right by Ireland, politically and economically. According to Elizabeth Longford, "though the Duke rarely declared emotional feelings for any subject or person explicitly, apart from the constitution and monarch, he was deeply and emotionally committed to Ireland. The strength of this feeling was shown by the amount of time he gave throughout his life to research and writing on possible solutions for Ireland's problems."[45]

Even this judicious assertion of Wellington's enduring if also impulsive commitment to Ireland, however, glosses over a number of complexities about the duke's own "Irishness," his relationship to Ireland over the course of his political career, and, more important for the purposes of my argument here, the protracted struggle between radically opposing political factions in Ireland and England to claim him as one of their own. In the end, the "unresolved dichotomies in the Duke's stance on Irish issues" were echoed by the unresolvable contradictions that materialized in the English and Irish presses in 1852.[46] The *Age* reacted with uncharacteristic violence to the *Galway Vindicator*'s provocative claim that the "noble passion of patriotism was a stranger to [Wellington's] rigid nature"[47] by challenging Irish editorialists to "confess that the Duke was neither of

Irish blood, nor Irish temperament," since "English blood and English temperament—not accidental birth—make Englishmen."[48] In response, the *Belfast Mercury* astutely located in such acrimonious taunts an intractable assumption about racial superiority, noting, "The subject is nothing less than a comparison of the superior physical qualities, and we believe all other qualities, of the Celt and Saxon. . . . Would any man or journalist dare to treat the most degraded and debased Negro in the same fashion?"[49]

Wellington's body became the terrain of struggle precisely because he could be legitimately embraced or rejected by both sides. The various qualities he was supposed to embody and perform, however, differed considerably depending on which side appropriated him. At various points in previous chapters, evidence of the hero's status in the Victorian imagination as the pattern of stoical duty and common sense has been presented to show how posthumous representations consistently returned to the conflation of Wellington and Englishness. According to one Victorian preacher, Wellington was to be "considered in the light of a national possession, in whom every Englishman owned a share."[50] But this possessive language suggested that ownership itself, however forcefully advertised as a privilege of the English, required a tireless refutation of competing claims. Wellington's positive attributes were proclaimed and guaranteed only through ceaseless proscription of the negative, of the un-Wellingtonian liabilities to which his reputation was evidently vulnerable. For the English, Irishness, like Frenchness, was a central and constitutive feature of censured otherness.

The *Age* was particularly virulent in its disputation of Wellington's Irishness, demanding in its most sarcastic tone that its "polite and gentlemanly friend," the editor at the *Galway Vindicator*, concede that Wellington "bore no Irish name, and cherished no Irish feelings." "Will not the *Vindicator* admit," the *Age* thundered, "that his progenitors on either side were pure English? . . . Was not the deceased soldier a thorough type of the hated Saxon? . . . Were not his unyielding energy, his high-souled honesty, his imperious sense of duty, his calm courage, and his love of truth,—were not all these low qualities Saxon to the bone?"[51] Of course, this battery of questions tells us more about the *Age*'s preconceptions about Irishness than it does about the actual qualities of that dubious entity, the

Saxon. The Celtic disposition was deemed an amalgamated negation of the Saxon's virtues: indolence, duplicity, irresponsibility, cowardice, and deception were, implicitly, Irish traits.

As Declan Kiberd observes, "If Ireland had never existed, the English would have invented it."[52] Wellington's funeral became yet another opportunity for England to reinvent its island neighbor as a means of asserting its own unique strengths and virtues. This reinvention, however, was articulated within a conventional language that had roots at least as far back as the late sixteenth century, when Edmund Spenser outlined an uncompromising program for Irish reform in his *View of the Present State of Ireland* (1596) and William Shakespeare amused playgoers with his mildly patronizing depiction of Captain Macmorris in *Henry V* (1599). English newspapers returned to "those traits of garrulity, pugnacity and a rather unfocused ethnic pride" that were presumed to be the essential characteristics of the Irishman.[53] In the process, they invented an image of the Napoleonic hero as fundamentally not-Irish, a man whose composure, good judgment, and quiet devotion to the English Crown marked him as everything the stage Irishman was not.

An especially telling instance of this typecasting occurred in the pages of *Punch* shortly after Wellington's death, an instance in which racial otherness was signaled through the periodical's exploitation of visual as well as linguistic characteristics that would have been recognizably "Celtic" in postfamine Britain. In *A Present from Galway*, "Paddy" emerges as, simultaneously, a belligerent, would-be antagonist and a parochial, impotent bumpkin (figure 6.1). *Punch* had never been an admirer of Wellington, as the next chapter will demonstrate, and was always ready to satirize his pretensions or impugn his political blunders. But by deriding the Irishman's desire, expressed in clichéd vernacular, to join in the "filliloo of the [Duke's] Funeral" by "comin over to London"—an "intintion" ultimately foiled by an "unforeseen combination of circumstances" (namely, his "want of the dhirty railway fare")—the paper tacitly participates in the depiction of the funeral as a cosmopolitan and very English affair, an event that makes of the stereotyped Irishman an appropriately excluded and ridiculous pretender. This "likeness" of a man who "would have [been] seen . . . in Fleet Street . . . on Thursday, November the Eighteenth, 1852, hurling defiance

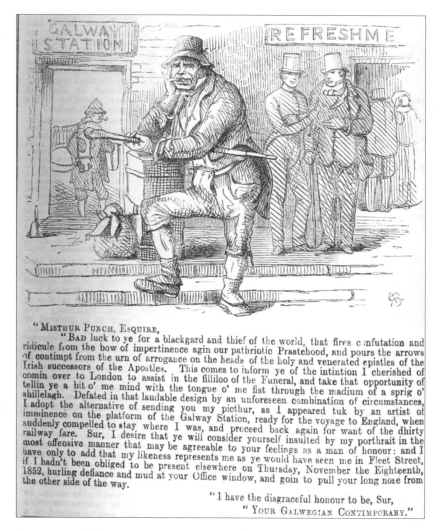

FIGURE 6.1 *A Present from Galway*, *Punch*, 3 October 1846.

and mud" if he had not been inhibited by his own imprudence, is the pictorial nadir of racial and cultural anxieties that had to be contained and managed in the wakes of both Wellington and the famine.

The "Galwegian Contimporary's" disaffection is, predictably, self-produced: he is a specimen of pugnacious vulnerability. In word and image, he constructs himself as caricature, blissfully unaware of the fact that his bravado and vanity are the source of bemused diversion for the reader—and, apparently, for the two gentlemen to the Irishman's left, whose smart clothes and genteel deportment indicate urbane Englishness. Their seemingly casual appearance in the background of the "picthur . . . tuk by an artist of imminence on the platform of the Galway Station" is, in fact, anything but coincidental. With their polished top hats and pressed tails, they serve as the respectable standard according to which the grimacing, broad-faced, simian Irishman's depravity can be judged. Their presence serves to illustrate Kiberd's argument that, when it came to depictions of the Irish through the English imagination, "if John Bull was industrious and reliable, Paddy was held to be indolent and contrary; if the former was mature and rational, the latter must be unstable and emotional."[54]

As a manifestation of this polarizing logic, the leering Irishman is also Wellington's repressed double, an atavistic figure invoked expressly to be dismissed. A throwback to a primitive and lower form of existence, this exemplary Irishman is the great duke's unspeakable alter ego, an example of racial perversion and devolution that must be repudiated. *Punch's* Irishman is not-Wellington, the malignant form of Irishness that the hero left behind unconditionally when he eschewed Ireland. *Punch's* cartoon thus demonstrates that, with the occasion of Wellington's funeral, "Ireland was [once again] . . . patented as not-England, a place whose peoples were, in many important ways, the very antithesis of their . . . rulers from overseas."[55]

The invention of racial differences essential to the constitution of antithetical English (Saxon and Protestant) and Irish (Celtic and Catholic) identities enabled highly reputable newspapers such as the *Morning Herald* to attack with the most opprobrious language the "sleek, sanctimonious, sinister-looking, and most fawning priestly parasites" of Ireland whom they blamed for fomenting anti-Wellington sentiment immediately after his death.[56] They also allowed *John Bull* to argue that its readers should not "wonder at the ingratitude with which the Irish Papists requite the boon of emancipation for which they are so largely indebted to him who has just been taken from us," since "black ingratitude is engrained [*sic*] in the Papist."[57] In both cases, the English press assumed an instinctive tendency on the part of the Irish to slavishly emulate the nefarious example set by their religious leaders, who emerged as a homogeneous, deceitful intelligentsia.

As I suggested earlier, however, the hero's death also provoked Irish nationalists to reconsider their country's ideological prerogatives with relation to the Wellington birthright and name and, consequently, to reinvent England as not-Ireland. Having accused Wellington of abandoning his native country to do merely "what he was paid for [by the English], and . . . nothing more,"[58] the *Galway Vindicator* declared that the Irish-born hero had, in turn, been largely ostracized on the day of the funeral by his bona fide compatriots: "In the pageant which accompanied him to the tomb, we have no part. At his departure it is for Ireland to lament, too; but not in such fashion. It is hers to mourn at a distance the hero who first drew breath on her bosom."[59] Willfully forgetting that the dead Wellington was no less Irish than he was on the day of his birth, the English deluded themselves into believing that they venerated their own best qualities as they revered the duke. The funeral was a deeply ironic affair; the *Vindicator* located in the posthumous Wellington worship an imaginative failure on the part of the English to comprehend that they were, in fact, exalting Irishness itself.

Like the *Freeman's Journal*, however, the *Vindicator* wanted it both ways. Wellington was indubitably an Irishman when that designation helped the newspaper to reveal the paradox of English mourners eulogizing a hero whose lineage was necessarily degraded by its associations with Ireland. But Wellington became an unspoken Englishman when the *Vindicator* found it convenient to let him stand implicitly as a type of English mendacity:

> It was not that [Wellington] was wonderful, but it was the Irishmen who fought under him—it was not his leading—but their following that elevated him to the pitch of glory. He had not wings, forsooth . . . that dullard of a Duke had nothing in his mind that soared. . . . The Duke had not so much dignity—so much nobility of mind as his own horse. . . . Your genuine Englishman . . . is a ruffian and a coward. They are a nation of cowards and ruffians who tread and trample on the weak, and cringe and truckle to the brave and powerful.[60]

If this maligning of Englishmen was an understandable, tit-for-tat reaction against the equally abusive anti-Irish invective discharged from London, the English press simply dismissed it as the lascivious dross of a hyperbolic race prone to self-contradiction. The *Morning Chronicle* noted that, fortunately, "the tone of these effusions was so utterly overstrained and morbid that their virulence defeated itself, and aroused at least as much contempt as indignation."[61]

But the *Chronicle*'s easy repudiation was ingenuous. Indignation and contempt were the anticipated reactions to any vigorous signs of Irish disaffection. In the wake of Wellington, the Irish press played to those racial preconceptions and prejudices held by the English, inciting already expected reactions to Irish ambitions through the use of intentionally incendiary language. In this way, the Irish reaffirmed their own radical otherness, declaring their autonomy by provoking a traditionally hostile English audience to once again articulate—to literally publish—its aversion to and concomitant difference from the Irish character. Kiberd's observation about the obligatory invention of Ireland therefore has its analogue: if England had never existed, the Irish would have invented it—in order to invent and reinvent themselves.

Arguably, then, Wellington did more for Irish solidarity once dead than when alive. His value in this regard reveals what Sarah Webster Goodwin and Elisabeth Bronfen have called "the dead body's peculiar power."[62] Wellington's posthumous "rebirth" through charged nationalist rhetoric demonstrated that "to give voice to the corpse, to represent the body, is in a sense to return it to life: the voice represents not so much the dead as the once living, juxtaposed with the needs of the yet living."[63] Those "overstrained" effusions about English cowardice and despotism, exemplified in the character and conduct of Wellington, ignited the defensive rancor of the English, who returned the venomous accusations with an ardor equal to that of their Irish antagonists. An ancillary effect of this backlash was that it served as an invitation to the Irish to publicize their indignation and alienation and, in the process, to articulate a narrative about Irishness with specific reference to the qualities of Wellington. Whether they appropriated or derided him, Irish newspapers, like their English counterparts, used the Wellington legend as a platform for nationalist self-fashioning.

The *Galway Vindicator*, as has been seen, was especially adept at arousing the fury of periodicals that would defend the English character. *Punch* was so "choked" by the accusations of its Irish rival that it published a companion piece to *A Present from Galway*, an essay decrying "An Irish Howl at a Hero's Wake." *Punch* portrayed the "invective" and "yelping" of that "false knave," the *Vindicator*'s editorialist, as "a little vain boasting—a spice of rhodomontade, [and] a smack of balderdash"—deplorably, the rhetorical weapons of choice for any "howling Paddy" predisposed to extravagant prating.[64] But by engaging the *Vindicator* on its own terms with acrid name-calling and chauvinist slurs, *Punch* was drawn into self-contradiction. By staunchly defending Wellington against the indignities of the Irish press, *Punch* temporarily abandoned its customary, sardonic attitude toward "The Dook," in effect acknowledging the potency of the *Vindicator*'s calumniations by so vigorously denouncing them. This is yet another example of the ways in which national cohesion was produced, however transiently, by the soldier-hero's commemoration. A unified front was required to repel outside provocations, and *Punch* redirected its satire away from domestic targets, rallying—along with surprising allies such as the *Times*, the *Morning Herald*, and the *Age*—under the sign of Englishness, a sign connoting, in this instance, the dignified and temperate grief of a people whose own solidarity was reinforced in proportion to the intensity of the assaults on Wellington's character.

In contrast, during *Punch*'s early years—roughly, the decade preceding Wellington's death—its satire at the expense of the duke was most consistently routed through badinage against the increasingly ubiquitous monuments, especially the equestrian statues, being planned or erected in his honor. Just as the *Age* would comment somewhat derisively on the "scores on scores" of Wellington images posted in the capital's shop windows after his death, *Punch*, in a whimsical essay of 1848 entitled "The Hero of a Hundred Statues," expressed its fear that London was fast becoming "a sort of livery stable, where the Hero of Waterloo and his horse are being constantly put up."[65] *Punch* punned on a deficiency it had long identified with and deplored in the elderly statesman, his tendency to "drag his heels" on issues of political and social reform:

> The Duke's head will soon be as familiar an object in the metropolis as the top of the monument or the dome of St. Paul's. . . . There is hardly a street where the Duke of Wellington may not be seen looking in at the top windows, or inhaling the smoke from the chimneys, or preparing to take a gentle trot over the tiles. . . . If we want a new site for a statue, we shall soon begin to find that "the Duke of Wellington's horse stops the way." For it must be remembered that the steed generally shares with his master in this great game of thoroughfare cribbage, and that if the former needs one yard for his head, the other requires at least two for his heels.[66]

In fact, the "great game" mentioned here had its own peculiar subtext, a story about two entwined commemorative acts that would have been familiar to *Punch*'s nineteenth-century readers. The title of *Punch*'s essay made farcical allusion to a hero-worshipping tradition that celebrated in poems and paintings the military successors of the semilegendary figure of Conn, an Irish king of the second century who was also called "the hero of a hundred fights." *Punch* thus also seemed to make a comical gibe at J. M. W. Turner's painting *The Hero of a Hundred Fights,* which immortalized the 1846 casting of Matthew Cotes Wyatt's enormous equestrian statue of Wellington placed at Hyde Park Corner. The final chapter turns to a closer examination of these examples of "high" memorial art to consider the ways in which a very different type of opposition—that of the public to works of art commemorating a long-dead hero—also contributed to the fabrication of the Wellington myth.

SEVEN

Epilogue

The Hyde Park Corner Controversy

IN 1881, the London Board of Works arranged to dismantle and move
the triumphal arch at Hyde Park Corner 105 yards southeast along
Constitution Hill in order to smooth the flow of congested traffic. When
it learned of the plan, the Royal Academy of Arts was quick to suggest
that the colossal memorial perched on top of Decimus Burton's 1828
landmark be permanently removed. The sixty-ton equestrian statue of
Wellington, represented as he might have appeared on the evening of
18 June 1815 toward the close of the Battle of Waterloo, mounted on his famous charger, Copenhagen, had been designed and cast by Matthew Cotes
Wyatt and positioned on Burton's arch in 1846 (figure 7.1).[1] The academy's
recommendation was acted upon with surprising alacrity. Wyatt's statue
was taken down and temporarily stored in a vacant space near Apsley
House while a government-appointed committee decided what to do with
it. In 1884, it was handed over to the military authorities, and the next year,
it was cut into small pieces, conveyed unceremoniously to Hampshire, and
reassembled on a large pedestal near All Saints Garrison Church in

FIGURE 7.1 *The Great Wellington Statue and Arch, Illustrated London News,* 21 November 1852.

Aldershot. "Today," F. Darrell Munsell observes, "almost hidden by trees, the Iron Duke languishes overlooking the Long Valley."[2] Burton's arch, in turn, continues to stand in isolated splendor at Hyde Park Corner. A busy ring road now cuts it off from pedestrian life and from Apsley House, upon which it and its massive fixture once cast an unmistakable shadow. Adrian Jones's comparatively discreet *Peace in a Quadriga* (1912) now graces the arch's pediment, conforming to Burton's original design and replacing a monument that for decades was at the center of a Victorian controversy about the nature and form of public memorialization.

The perseverance of this controversy from the moment of the statue's conception in 1838 to its rather undignified removal suggests that dissension was only tangentially related to utilitarian concerns about increased traffic and the need for urban modification. The latter served as convenient excuses for the unseating of a work that had for years been part of a drama about appropriate commemorative practice. The Royal Academy's aversion, therefore, can be situated within a history of general contention and recrimination about Wyatt's statue that helps to explain the work's plagued aesthetic legacy and the pervasive acclamation that greeted its removal from an important metropolitan thoroughfare.[3]

If present-day readers are at all familiar with the controversy, it is probably through the satirical efforts of William Makepeace Thackeray, who played an early and memorable role in the statue's unfortunate history by verbally and visually lampooning "that hideous equestrian monster" as a preeminent example of the "sorts of humbugs and falsenesses and pretensions" that occupy that "very vain, wicked, foolish place," Vanity Fair.[4] In the novel *Vanity Fair*, as Mary Hammond has forcefully argued, "the worlds of 1815 and 1847–48 [are] in constant public dialogue."[5] Nowhere is this confrontation between the Napoleonic past and the writer's present more visible than in Thackeray's illustration for the cover of the novel's first monthly part (1847), in which the moralizing narrator, dressed as a clown and standing on a barrel, pontificates before the rogues and wenches of Vanity Fair. The clown-preacher's left hand points directly to Wyatt's gigantic statue, which shares the London skyline with Nelson's column, whose famous denizen stands comically on his head. By alluding pictorially to the city's fondness for casting the nation's heroes in bronze, Thackeray hints at the folly of humanity itself; as one of many Napoleonic allusions and episodes in the novel, this first of Thackeray's "pen and pencil sketches of English society" serves to "deepen our sense of mankind's hopeless obtuseness and futility."[6]

This chapter revisits some of the most contentious episodes in the curious metropolitan saga so strikingly caricatured by Thackeray. Part of my interest is simply to account for "the greatest sculptural fiasco of the 19th century, attended by almost an excess of press coverage," in this way drawing to a close my discussion of Wellington's symbolic value, which, by the 1880s, was vested primarily in sculptural and textual monuments rather than in the immediate legacy of the man himself.[7] I also want to demonstrate, however, that the statue's ignominious removal represents a clash between an aesthetics of the sublime and a carefully fostered mythology of celebrity, an argument that returns us to the question of Wellington's reputation and its relation to his singular virtues—particularly, to the ideas of Wellingtonian Englishness and duty.

Two dissonant claims about the nature of sublimity come into competition in the debate about the statue. On the one hand, Wyatt's monument was an unprecedented achievement in terms of scale, a singular expression of that innovative aesthetic, the "industrial sublime." As Gerald Finley has shown, the industrial sublime had its roots in the late eighteenth-century art of painters such as Joseph Wright and Philippe Jacques de Loutherbourg, who were fascinated with the flaring factories and noisome mills that complemented the natural sublimity of the darkened and blasted environments in which they often stood.[8] Although in 1790, Immanuel Kant had prohibited humanmade objects from belonging to the category of the "true" sublime, arguing in *The Critique of Judgement* that "the sublime, in the strict sense of the word, cannot be contained in any sensuous form, but rather concerns ideas of reason [of] which . . . no adequate presentation . . . is possible . . . because the mind has been incited to abandon sensibility, and employ itself upon ideas involving higher finality,"[9] this limitation in no way impinged upon the aesthetic aspirations that lay behind Wyatt's statue. Kant would perhaps argue that the Wellington monument could not achieve the highest form of the sublime, which is only to be found in nature "in such of its phenomena as in their intuition convey the idea of their infinity."[10] However, there can be little doubt that Wyatt's adaptation of Burton's arch as a pedestal for a statue "said to be the largest in the world" was a sublime experiment, even if it ultimately lapsed into the ridiculous.[11] "That is sublime in comparison with which all else is small,"[12] Kant observed, and certainly no other statue of the period was comparable to Wyatt's in terms of sheer size.

On the other hand, Wellington's popular if also inevitably disputed reputation as a patriot and dutiful servant of the Crown was distinctive for its emphasis on his defensive brilliance, moral candor, and unremitting conscientiousness, what might be called the "practical sublime" of the English character he was believed to manifest. In a language that by this point is familiar and predictable, one eulogist averred that "[Wellington] had, combined in himself, in a singular degree, the national qualities on which the English people pride themselves, clear practical honesty of intellect, patience, probity, fidelity of character."[13] These unexceptional "national qualities" were contradicted by Wyatt's grandiose statue, which was condemned in many quarters as an ostentatious and implicitly un-English addition to the urban landscape.

All of London seemed to have an opinion on the statue, but few of the critics exhibited much generosity. Indeed, excoriation was immediate and enduring and was not limited to the general public. The Wellington Memorial Committee, for example, formed in 1838 under the instigation of Common Councillor Thomas Bridge Simpson and chaired by the Duke of Rutland, became infamous for internal squabbling. When a working subcommittee selected Wyatt rather than Richard Westmacott as sculptor, the Marquess of Anglesey wrote to Prime Minister William Lamb, Viscount Melbourne, asking Her Majesty's Government to suspend a decision on the arch. Melbourne's capitulation to this request led him into hot water, and he backed off, but not before the *Morning Chronicle* very publicly lambasted Anglesey and the prime minister for their meddling.

Viscount Canning, chief commissioner of woods and forests, ran into similar difficulties when, just months before the memorial was to be erected on Burton's arch and under pressure from government, he proposed to locate the statue either in Waterloo Place or on Horse Guards Parade rather than at Hyde Park Corner. Rutland strenuously defied Canning's wish. The colossal work was removed from Wyatt's foundry on 27 September, more than three months after the date originally planned for its unveiling—18 June, Waterloo Day. A tricky evacuation required demolition of a wall and removal of the foundry's roof. It was pulled along the Harrow Road by twenty-nine horses on a specially designed, twenty-ton car in a great military parade that lasted one and a half hours, accompanied by bands playing "See the Conquering Hero Comes" and led by large detachments of Life Guards, Fusiliers, Grenadiers, and Coldstreams (figure 7.2), surely one of the most eccentric sights witnessed in nineteenth-century London.

Obviously, however, "one could not drag the largest statue in the world through the streets of London, and erect it at a busy crossroads, in secrecy."[14] Although Rutland worried in a letter to Wyatt that "if we make a great Parade on the occasion of fixing the Statue on the Arch . . . we

FIGURE 7.2 Procession of the Wellington statue, *Illustrated London News*, 3 October 1846.

should run the risk of being laughed at,"[15] the subcommittee's final decision to organize a grand procession embraced the inevitable, and no attempt was made to shy away futilely from display. On the contrary, the procession of a monolithic statue to such astonishing fanfare was an exemplary instance of what Thomas Richards calls the early "Victorian taste for spectacle," a "rhetorical mode of amplification and excess that came to pervade and structure public and private life in the nineteenth century."[16] Wyatt's "wonderful work" quickly became the focal point of a spectacle staged for the sake of spectacle itself. The ostensible subject of the statue, Wellington, was in this sense superfluous, at least at the moment of observers' initial, bedazzled encounter with his gigantic image.[17] "The certainty that the means of spectacular representation signified anything in particular had disappeared," Richards claims, "and increasingly it was the means themselves that mattered. And the means were industrial."[18] As reports on the statue's progress in London-based newspapers such as the *Illustrated London News,* the *Art-Union,* and the *Morning Post* had become more frequent in the early months of 1846, Victorian spectators were increasingly eager to witness for themselves the labor being undertaken to produce the still inconceivable leviathan.[19] In Wyatt's studio, they could gaze upon sections of the prodigious monument long before it was fully assembled; the process was transformed from mere curiosity to spectacle in its own right and for its own end (figure 7.3). From the moment its mold was shaped, the statue was triumphed chiefly as the product of new industrial techniques, which included unconventional relations of production. The *ILN,* for example, informed its readers that more than forty tons of metal were used for horse and rider, that the group was fashioned on a giant turntable weighing nearly as much as the statue itself, and that more than thirty men were employed on the bronze at any one time.

The odd parade, too, recast the mundane necessity of freighting the statue from one point to another, turning it into a spectacular celebration of industrial prowess. Like the Great Exhibition but even more explicitly, it served as a kind of trial run for Wellington's own funeral six years later, another graphic and melodramatic spectacle. Considered side by side, the *ILN*'s high-quality engravings of the Wellington statue's parade in figure 7.2 and of the duke's funeral procession in the Strand (figure 5.3) look as if they could depict different sections of the same pageant. There is little to differentiate them in terms of composition: they share an elevated, encompassing point of view; they masterfully create a sense of dramatic perspective; and they commemorate implicitly London itself—its dignified buildings, its constabulary, its well-ordered crowds, in short, its facility to organize and host such major events.

Through its coverage of events such as the funeral and the Wellington statue's parade, the *ILN* adeptly marketed its own unique position as the nation's first virtually encyclopedic pictorial chronicle. With its commencement, the newspaper had proclaimed, "the public [would] have henceforth under their glance, and within their grasp, the very form and presence of events as they transpire, in all their substantial reality, and with evidence visual as well as circumstantial."[20] By 1846, the *ILN*'s reputation was such that it was invited unofficially to document in words and pictures the Wellington statue's construction: "By [September 1846], London was reaching a pitch of excitement and anticipation concerning the mammoth.

FIGURE 7.3 *Mr Wyatt's Atelier, Illustrated London News*, 11 July 1846.

The *Illustrated London News*, allowed a peep into the Wyatts' studio and foundry, engraved views of the work, as well as illustrations of how it was assumed the statue would look upon the arch, and these had been appearing in that periodical for some weeks."[21] The *ILN* therefore prepared the public for the statue's appearance. More important, it functioned as a salutary agent for Wyatt's monument, cultivating for it a positive image and doing much to temper the public's initial reception.

By the time the statue was raised and fixed on 29 September, then, it had already been amply featured in the press. But it had also been subject to appraisals considerably more abusive than anything that appeared in the *ILN*, which took no umbrage with the statue or with the £30,000 contracted to Wyatt for its creation. The monument suffered the most importunate obloquy on the pages of the still-radical *Punch*. While the *ILN* was busy at the work of posterity, assembling its pictorial record of the statue's construction as part of its mandate to provide a complete register of significant metropolitan events, *Punch* lived up to its early Tory- and Wellington-baiting reputation by ridiculing the statue as a "brazen monster" that appeared "like a night-mare amidst the dense mass of people" gathered to watch its emergence from Wyatt's studio.[22] Over the course of the statue's thirty-seven years on the triumphal arch, *Punch* was to publish a series of satirical illustrations and essays about the colossus, many of them of a comically speculative nature, all determined to impress upon readers that the statue was a "gigantic triumph of bad taste over public opinion."[23] Columns with titles such as "Reflections on the Duke's Statue" and "The Rise and Fall of the Wellington Statue" became semiregular components of the paper in the months leading up to the monument's completion ("It seems that small dinner parties have been given inside the horse. . . . Why not let out the statue in lodgings?").[24] Few images were more exuberant than the 1846 engraving of the statue's extraordinary transportation to Hyde Park Corner (figure 7.4)—a send-up both of the anachronistic imperial progress and of the irony-free treatment the parade received in periodicals such as the *ILN*. And none were as delightfully malicious as an 1883 picture of the deposed and suddenly animated statue of Wellington, eyebrows arched incredulously at an unexpected humiliation that Mr. Punch evidently enjoys, albeit with a dubious gesture of respect (figure 7.5).

Punch's decision to make the latter picture the cover image for its annual volume indicates that Wyatt's statue had become firmly identified in the popular imagination with London's architectural follies: by 1883, the statue was presumed to be an immediately recognizable symbol of metropolitan extravagance. In the preceding years, it had become a primary target for *Punch*'s mockery. An object of ridicule in no fewer than forty editorial pieces and engravings throughout 1846 alone, the statue became emblematic of the paper itself, a kind of secondary signature piece. In fact, in the months leading up to the statue's completion and for a brief period after its erection, the duke's prominently beaked nose competed directly with Punch's humped back as a visual signifier for the paper's self-declared mission to be "speaking for all England" with a tone of mild satire.[25] The site chosen for the monument was especially egregious in the judgment of a periodical that viewed itself as a patron of urbane tastes.[26]

FIGURE 7.4 *The Progress of the Welling-ton Statue,* Punch, 2 October 1846.

FIGURE 7.5 *Punch,* title page to vol. 84, 30 June 1883.

Professional academicians, in turn, condemned the statue's placement on the arch. The Royal Institute of British Architects invoked classical precedent, arguing that such massive objects belong on ground-level plinths. Burton agreed, fearing that his arch would be reduced to "the role of an insignificant pedestal."[27] Failing to save his masterpiece from the offense, he set aside £2000 in his will to have the statue removed. In similar vein, when Wyatt's plans for the statue were initially communicated, the anonymous author of "Reflections in Rhyme, on the Wellington Memorial" contended that the duke's appointment as a mounted soldier was an implicit challenge to royal authority. "Let him stand," reasoned the poet,

> The bridle of his charger in his hand,
> Ready to mount at the first trumpet's sound,
> But to defend, not trample on the crown'd;
> While on the arch, commanding war to cease,
> Victoria sits enthroned, a Queen of Peace.[28]

The queen herself did not appear anxious to displace Wellington in this way. She did, however, find it necessary to assuage the duke's chagrin over the threatened removal of the statue shortly after a three-week trial period for its placement on the arch had concluded. In August 1846, she had written to Lord John Russell, regretting that she was "bound by her word . . . [to] allow the Statue to go up, however bad the appearance of it will be."[29] When Wellington, writing to the queen with typical third-person self-reference, "first heard of the intention to remove the statue from the pedestal on which it had been placed, he was apprehensive that the measure might be misconstrued and misrepresented in this country as well as abroad."[30] Victoria responded to the duke's concerns in a letter to Lord Palmerston, explaining that "although she had thought that another pedestal would have been more suitable for *this* statue, and that the Arch might have been more becomingly ornamented in honour of the Duke than by the statue *now* upon it, she has given immediate direction that the Statue should remain in its present situation, and only regrets that this monument should be so unworthy of the great personage to whose honour it has been erected."[31] Like *Punch,* Victoria did not provide any specific rationale for this dismissal of the monument as unworthy, noting merely that it looked "bad." What might have been the basis for her aversion? Was she simply echoing the sentiments of informed observers who had spoken out against the monument as an enormity unsuitable for Burton's arch?

There is good reason to believe that the queen would have been predisposed to consider the statue a fundamentally incongruous addition to the arch, a result of prevailing notions about what constituted appropriate memorial practice in sculpture. The influence of the Royal Commission upon the early Victorians' understanding of sculptural merit, for example, would have cultivated the idea that the statue was incompatible with its new base, primarily because of its size. As secretary, Sir Charles Eastlake had written persuasively in the commission's third report (1844) about the "general principles (applicable to all the arts of design) of proportion, breadth, gradation of quantities, and contrast," contending that true excellence in sculpture lay in the study and emulation of the ancients, who were, most notably, masters of the first-listed attribute, proportion.[32] A letter from an anonymous "Inhabitant of May Fair" to the *Builder* shortly after the statue was raised illustrates how seriously Wyatt and the Wellington Memorial Committee were seen to have strayed from the protocols of symmetry:

> Incongruity . . . must always cause pain in the beholder, as is but too ostensibly demonstrated . . . by the equestrian statue upon Burton's archway, on Constitution Hill. The disproportion of the one to the other—the statue to the pedestal (the arch)—is infinitely greater than I had anticipated prior to the elevation; and as that disproportion so overpowers the pedestal, now that the large timbers hide portions of its form, how much more glaring and offensive to good taste must it be when denuded of them, and its full extent of size shall remain in no degree concealed?[33]

Whereas Eastlake, like the *Builder*'s correspondent, emphasized the importance of proportion, poet and critic Francis Turner Palgrave complained that most British sculpture had "no real hold on people" because it indulged in "mechanical trick or mechanical grandeur."[34] Taken as a barometer of such opinions, Victoria's reaction would therefore indicate that the statue's ignominy and ultimate eviction had to do with metonymic failure—Wyatt's overmagnification of his subject matter and his dedication to the display of "mechanical grandeur" over a memorialization complimentary to Burton's arch and to Wellington himself.

This is to say that Wyatt substituted vast physical size for an appropriate reminder of what I earlier called Wellington's incipient position within the pantheon of British war heroes. It was during the 1840s that the still-spry septuagenarian came to be "regarded as the living embodiment of disinterested infallibility": "The Wellington who had spent most of his life commanding armies was unsuited, whether by temperament or habit, from managing political men. . . . When the mists of animosity [had] lifted they reveal[ed] that figure so familiar from countless busts and portraits: the Duke, the national hero, an institution, almost a department of state."[35] From the heavily decried, antireform, retrogressive High Tory, despoiler of the Conservative Party's aspirations, Wellington became, during the late 1840s and early 1850s, Britain's Grand Old Man.

The Wyatt statue confronted this legacy with hapless audacity. As Alison Yarrington remarks, its "awkward profile against the sky, the lack of close resemblance to Copenhagen and the noise generated by the wind in the bronze plumes of the Duke's hat all acted to reduce the sublime conception of the project to the level of public nuisance."[36] In this sense, the Wyatt statue represented an extension of what Yarrington punningly calls Wellington's "Achilles Heel," his already vexed relationship with public art in the wake of Waterloo that saw numerous proposals for large-scale, classically inspired monuments to British war heroes.[37] Wyatt's Wellington met a fate that, for a time, also seemed certain to doom Richard Westmacott's *Achilles* statue, unveiled in 1822 at the southeast corner of Hyde Park immediately behind Apsley House, financed by the Ladies of England as a tribute to Wellington and forged, symbolically, from enemy cannon taken at the Battles of Salamanca, Vitoria, Toulouse, and Waterloo. John Harris's 1844 aquatint *A View in Hyde Park* alludes wittily to the physical incongruity between the brawny "Achilles" and the benign, elderly duke, who makes a characteristic touch of his hat in apparent salute to this egregious memorial to himself (figure 7.6). Most Londoners were

FIGURE 7.6 *A View in Hyde Park*, by John Harris, after H. de Baubrawa, 1844. ©
National Portrait Gallery, London.

confounded by the eighteen-foot *Achilles*. Its heavy allusiveness and con-
sequent ambiguity made it vulnerable to the widest possible interpretation. Further, its muscular near nudity failed to speak appropriately to the
reputation of Wellington, a man Samuel Smiles was to laud for his unfailing equanimity, "clear discernment and strong common sense."[38]

Like this now-entrenched characterization of Wellington as the
constrained and hence arch-English duke, *Achilles* has survived. Initial
hostility, however, illustrated what Yarrington calls "a gap between the
highly-tuned aesthetic discourse of art and those more immediate and
broader-based concerns of the public."[39] Munsell says something similar
about Wyatt's equestrian colossus. Controversy over the statue, he argues,
represented a struggle between three factious groups: Wellington's friends
and supporters, who were determined to honor his military achievements
and incorporate a memorial into the imperial capital of London; the

growing, antimilitaristic middle classes of midcentury; and the academically trained prosecutors and defenders of high art, whose sensibilities were at odds with those of the general public.

At the center of this controversy, as I have observed, lay the issue of the compatibility of Wyatt's bronze icon with what might be called the iconic reputation of Wellington himself from the early 1840s, the gradual "fixing" of the Iron Duke in the public imagination and memory as, simultaneously, the century's greatest war hero and the Crown's most loyal but also unpretentious servant. Wellington's embodiment of Englishness and the practical sublime has perhaps most notably been acclaimed by Smiles, who takes the duke as a supreme example of those "men of large and comprehensive minds, capable of action on the very largest scale"— "Men of Business."[40] Smiles repeatedly applauds Wellington's "indomitable firmness" and his distinction as a leader who, whether on the battlefield or in Parliament, "provided for every contingency" by attending scrupulously to details.[41] As I have already illustrated, the most popular Wellington mythology turned the hero of Waterloo into a soldier and statesman identified chiefly with the peculiarly English virtue of duty. The rather abstract good of Wellingtonian duty became for an admirer such as Smiles an expression of his hero's decidedly un-Bonapartean yet nevertheless "*sublime* patience and self-control."[42] For Henry Thomas Braithwaite, whose turgid *Ode* of 1852 lamented Wellington's death, the deceased prime minister invariably "spake th' inexorable 'must,'" and his spirit was appealed to apostrophically as the dispenser of sublime wisdom under national duress:

> And if the day accursed arise,
> When deeds of wrong pollute the scene
> Where once thou counselled'st sublime;
> If e'er our country, fallen in crime,
> Shall shun, as a reproof, they name,—
> Rise, O dead warrior, from thy tomb!
> Rise like a present doom!
> Rise with a thousand years of fame
> And in the senate sit thee down.[43]

And yet, even before Wyatt's statue was erected on Burton's arch, it was clear that its sublime conception failed to result in a monument that appropriately reflected what was rapidly becoming the hegemonic image of a sublimely dutiful hero. "The statue of the Duke of Wellington on the arch in Piccadilly," the *London Review* declared, speaking with finality and conviction on behalf of all discriminating Londoners, "was the ugliest thing" in the city, singularly deplorable even when considered side by side with other "prominent deformities of modern London."[44]

Aspiring too boldly toward the gargantuan and unparalleled in size by other such monuments in the capital, Wyatt's statue seemed to pay tribute to the ego of its creator rather than to the increasingly popular distinction of the subject it represented; in this sense, it unintentionally fixed the wrong reputation. It was too big in at least two senses, threatening to overwhelm (by deflecting attention away from) not only the triumphal arch on which it was placed but also the popular image of the man most biographers and apologists were trying to affirm in the service of England and Englishness—the archetype of candid masculinity and unassuming fidelity, the supreme exemplar of what Charles Greville, in his tribute to the duke, called "severe truthfulness" complemented by "an ever-abiding sense of duty and obligation."[45]

This deflection can be fruitfully interrogated by attending to a contradiction between a "sublime conception" other than the one to which Yarrington refers—that of J. M. W. Turner's late and underexamined painting, *The Hero of a Hundred Fights* (figure 7.7)—and the material result of the industrial process it celebrates. *The Hero* is an 1845 reworking of a canvas painted sometime between 1800 and 1810, and it offers a dramatic portrayal of the moment during casting when the Wellington statue's mold was removed. The original painting was uniformly dark in color and documented the operations of now-obscure industrial machinery. Turner's alterations of the image, especially through the addition of the fiery light on the left, transformed it so that, as Finley points out, the painting now "makes a pronounced commemorative statement."[46] It focuses on the furnace fire itself, the scene of genesis depicted as a "violent vortex of swirling light spiraling out from a white-hot centre" that J. Hillis Miller has identified as an elemental feature in the painter's landscapes.[47] Whereas the sun

FIGURE 7.7 *The Hero of a Hundred Fights*, by J. M. W. Turner, 1810 (?), reworked 1845. © Tate, London 2002.

is most often the source of this light in Turner's grand, mythic-historical compositions, in *The Hero,* viewers are confronted with what Miller calls "humankind's defiant challenge to the sun, the making of a second sun, a Promethean stealing of fire." If we accept Miller's thesis that "Turner's project as a painter was to create out of paint a second sun that would be not an imitation of light, but a light-source itself,"[48] then the blast furnace of this late canvas represents yet a third remove and something of an anomaly within Turner's oeuvre—a tribute to a tribute of greatness, wherein one artist commemorates another artist's act of commemoration and, in the process, extols technological innovation. Finley has therefore argued that Wellington is only "indirectly the subject of this painting."[49] That very indirection evokes the defining qualities of an aesthetic for which Turner is widely celebrated as the most accomplished nineteenth-century practitioner, the industrial sublime: visual abstruseness created by the startling effects of light and shade; the veiled malevolence of an object that defies clear distinction; the relative proximity of the viewer to this scene of formidable creation; and the remarkable energy and expression of power vested in the process itself.

Imperfectly visible as an imposing shadow against a luminous background, the Wellington statue is immortalized as an always-about-to-be-completed artifact: the painting revels in the energy and power of industrial creation and is endlessly suggestive about what will emerge. Incompletion, like indirection, signals the sublime in this tribute to contemporary history. Through such practiced vagaries, the painting demonstrates its exemplary patronage to Edmund Burke's treatise on the sublime, wherein obscurity, vastness of dimension hinting at the infinite, intense color, and bright light "such . . . as that of the sun" combine to produce sensations of dread and awe.[50] They also enable a kind of interpretive latitude amenable to the ways in which Wellington's own military and political reputation was being contested, amended, and increasingly purified at midcentury. Once it emerged from the blast furnace, however, the statue forfeited the evocative promise of the painting and was quickly judged to be an incongruous tribute to its heroic subject.

The origins of this particular incongruity, as I have argued, can be located in the exceptional elevation of Wellington's duty, so that it became a kind of fetish, an admirable trait that took on a life of its own in narrative characterizations of the duke's defining virtues. Wyatt's colossal statue, however, is part of the cult of the extraordinary personality. With its striking pose—an undaunted and composed Wellington gesturing with his spyglass during a final moment of crisis in an epic battle—it promotes for the duke the role of the autonomous and uninhibited commander at a time when the press, biographers, and artists were diligently constructing him as the Crown's most loyal servant. Wyatt misconstrued magnitude for the equivalent of true sublimity, and as a result, he produced what *Punch,* with instinctive perspicacity, called a "brazen monster."

The final word in the debate about the statue might most effectively go to Kant, whose uncharacteristically succinct remarks on heroic sculpture bespeak a fundamental contradiction at the heart of any such colossal enterprise: "An object is *monstrous* where by its size defeats the end that forms its concept. The *colossal* is the mere presentation of a concept which is almost too great for presentation, i.e. borders on the relatively monstrous."[51] With its size defeating the end, or what the correspondent to the *Builder* called overpowering disproportion, Wyatt's Wellington was, perhaps, doomed from the outset to excoriation and exile in the provinces.

The last word on Wellington, however, has not and will never be spoken—a prediction made in confidence because, as I have attempted to illustrate throughout this book, Wellington's life and death form chapters in a "still-developing national epic defined fundamentally in terms of military achievement," an epic that is under continual pressure to modify the hero's reputation, demonstrating, in turn, that the "heroic image [is] necessarily reworked into new shapes and significances" in response to shifting conjunctions between cultural imaginaries and the broader, national-popular culture.[52] This is an argument I have made at various points in this study and that serves as its conclusion.

Heroic reputations and indeed the very idea of heroism are constituted within a discursive field that is defined by the struggle and difference that attend language itself. With Wellington, we have seen numerous examples of the "reshaping of events" through which the dead hero is "located as the product of a . . . coherent story of heroic character-building."[53] The duke continues to be reshaped in response to the contingencies and requirements of the present day, even while a vast majority of the recent biographies display their indebtedness, whether consciously or not, to Herbert Maxwell's strain of serene veneration. Thus, the Wellington literature today retains, more or less unaltered, the legend of the unconquered duke, the brilliant military tactician and England's most worthy son, even when it attempts to account for the role of narrative in the fabrication of such inspirational stories. Acknowledging that much "may be said for or against him," examples of such literature ultimately make the familiar declaration that Wellington, "as a soldier and commander, [was] the greatest . . . this country—or perhaps any other—has produced."[54] My interest here has not been to counter this common assessment in order to assert a less flattering and more "accurate" appraisal but to illuminate a few of the narrative and pictorial strategies used by Wellington commemorators interested in making their own contribution to the myth of the mid-nineteenth century's most acclaimed paragon of Englishness.

NOTES

Introduction

1. After the title of George Morey's biography (London: Frederick Muller, 1967).

2. George P. Landow, *Victorian Types, Victorian Shadows: Biblical Typology in Victorian Literature, Art, and Thought* (Boston and London: Routledge and Kegan Paul, 1980), 145.

3. A. C. Charity, *Events and Their Afterlife: The Dialectics of Christian Typology in the Bible and Dante* (Cambridge: Cambridge University Press, 1966), 1.

4. *Times* (London), 18 September 1852, 4.

5. Cornelia D. J. Pearsall, "Burying the Duke: Victorian Mourning and the Funeral of the Duke of Wellington," *Victorian Literature and Culture* 27, no. 2 (1999): 377–78.

6. *Examiner* (London), 20 November 1852, 740. Notably, both Tennyson and Martin Tupper (1810–1899)—the latter a "prolific author who clothed evangelical truisms in colourful metaphors, pleasing metre and comfortable words" and who was at the height of his now-forgotten fame in 1852 (Neville Thompson, "Immortal Wellington: Literary Tributes to the Hero," in *Wellington Studies III*, ed. C. M. Woolgar [Southampton, UK: Hartley Institute, 1999], 262)—also composed topical poems on the occasion of the opening of the Great Exhibition, examined in chapter 2. Copies of the laureate's and his lesser-known contemporary's poems sold well following both midcentury events.

7. John Marius Wilson, *A Memoir of Field-Marshal the Duke of Wellington: With Interspersed Notices of His Principal Associates in Council, and Companions and Opponents in Arms*, 2 vols. (London: A. Fullerton, n.d.), 2:606.

8. Herbert Maxwell, *The Life of Wellington: The Restoration of the Martial Power of Great Britain*, 2nd ed., 2 vols. (London: Sampson Low, Marston and Co., 1900), 1:xii.

9. Walter B. May, *A Panegyric in Honour of the Duke of Wellington* (Taunton, UK: Frederick May, 1854), 34, 24–25.

10. *Age* (London), 25 September 1852, 4.

11. Maxwell, *Life*, 1:5.

12. G. W. Conder, *Duty and Destiny, or, the Ruling Ideas of Wellington and Napoleon* (London: Hamilton, Adams, 1852), 5.

13. Nigel Llewellyn, *The Art of Death: Visual Culture in the English Death Ritual, 1500–1800* (London: Reaktion, 1991), 60, 93.

14. Frank Turner, *Contesting Cultural Authority: Essays in Victorian Intellectual Life* (Cambridge: Cambridge University Press, 1993), 248.

15. *Leeds Mercury,* 18 September 1852, 4.

16. See Joseph A. Kestner, *Masculinities in Victorian Painting* (Aldershot, UK: Scolar, 1995): "The construction of masculinity that came most readily to the minds of Victorian artists was that derived from the mythology of Greece and Rome. The classical world and its literature had created paradigms of male behaviours which the world of nineteenth-century Britain was able to remould, refashion and reconstruct for the purposes of advancing the masculine ideologies of Victorian culture" (48).

17. Leonard Cooper, *The Age of Wellington: The Life and Times of the Duke of Wellington, 1769–1852* (London: Macmillan, 1964), v.

18. Neville Thompson, *Wellington after Waterloo* (London: Routledge and Kegan Paul, 1986), 7.

19. A. M. Close, *National Obsequies Sanctioned by Holy Writ. A Sermon* (London: Hatchard, 1852), 8.

20. Nicholas Michell, *The Burial of Wellington: An Elegiac and Tributary Poem* (London: William Tegg, 1852), ll.43–46, 69–76.

21. See, respectively, Pat Jalland, "Death, Grief, and Mourning in the Upper-Class Family, 1860–1914," in *Death, Ritual, and Bereavement,* ed. Ralph Houlbrooke (London: Routledge, 1989), 185, and Ruth Richardson, "Why Was Death So Big in Victorian Britain?" in *Death, Ritual,* 115. It has also been called an event that saw "the theme of Death and the Hero . . . celebrated with . . . a sublime lack of proportion" (John Morley, *Death, Heaven and the Victorians* [Pittsburgh, PA: University of Pittsburgh Press, 1971], 80) and, more generously if less definitively, as "the greatest spectacle that the Victorian world had seen" (Harry Garlick, "The Staging of Death: Iconography and the State Funeral of the Duke of Wellington," *Australian Journal of Art* 9 [1991]: 63).

22. N. Thompson, "Immortal Wellington."

23. Iain Pears, "The Gentleman and the Hero: Wellington and Napoleon in the Nineteenth Century," in *Myths of the English,* ed. Roy Porter (Cambridge: Polity, 1992), 216–36.

24. John Wolffe, *Great Deaths: Grieving, Religion, and Nationhood in Victorian and Edwardian Britain* (Oxford: Oxford University Press, 2000).

25. Pearsall, "Burying the Duke," 371, 389.

26. Ibid., 365. Wolffe, in fact, issues a challenge taken up expressly in the present work, arguing that several of the cases he examines for their "exceptional prominence" would "be worthy of a book in their own right," meriting more detailed analysis than his own study gives them; see Wolffe, *Great Deaths,* 8, 9. The author looks at the deaths of Wellington, Prince Albert, David Livingston, Disraeli, General Gordon, Prince Albert Victor, the Duke of Clarence, Gladstone, Victoria, and King Edward VII.

27. Gail Turley Houston, *Royalties: The Queen and Victorian Writers* (Charlottesville and London: University Press of Virginia, 1999), 3.

28. Adrienne Munich, *Queen Victoria's Secrets* (New York: Columbia University Press, 1996), 7.

29. Stephen C. Behrendt, *Royal Mourning and Regency Culture: Elegies and Memorials of Princess Charlotte* (Houndmills, UK: Macmillan, 1997), 33.

30. Munich, *Victoria's Secrets*, 2.

31. See Michael Greenhalgh, "The Funeral of the Duke of Wellington," *Apollo* 98 (September 1973): 224: "It was . . . appropriate that [Wellington's and Nelson's] funerals should resemble each other. Thus Nelson lay in state at Greenwich, was transferred to the Admiralty before the procession was borne through the streets on a chassis decked out to represent the prow and stern of *Victory*. . . . St. Paul's was also blacked out for the occasion, and the ceremony was by all accounts interminable, taking place in an atmosphere suffocatingly stuffy thanks to the candle-smoke."

32. See Wolffe, *Great Deaths*, 287–88.

33. Ibid., 188.

34. Elizabeth Longford, *Victoria R. I.* (London: Pan, 1964), 706.

35. *Scotsman* (Edinburgh), 22 September 1852, 4.

36. William H. Epstein, *Recognizing Biography* (Philadelphia: University of Pennsylvania Press, 1987), 145.

37. Laura Marcus, *Auto-biographical Discourses: Theory, Criticism, Practice* (Manchester, UK: Manchester University Press, 1994), 25.

38. Martin Stannard, "The Necrophiliac Art?" in *The Literary Biography: Problems and Solutions*, ed. Dale Salwak (Iowa City: University of Iowa Press, 1996), 32.

39. John Glavin, *After Dickens: Reading, Adaptation and Performance* (Cambridge: Cambridge University Press, 1999), 4.

40. Peter Metcalf and Richard Huntington, *Celebrations of Death: The Anthropology of Mourning Ritual* (Cambridge: Cambridge University Press, 1991), 25.

Chapter 1: Aftereffects

1. Graham Dawson, *Soldier Heroes: British Adventure, Empire and the Imagining of Masculinities* (London: Routledge, 1994), 1.

2. Herbert Sussman, *Victorian Masculinities: Manhood and Masculine Poetics in Early Victorian Literature and Art* (Cambridge: Cambridge University Press, 1995), 8.

3. Dennis W. Allen, "Young England: Muscular Christianity and the Politics of the Body in *Tom Brown's School Days*," in *Muscular Christianity: Embodying the Victorian Age*, ed. Donald E. Hall (Cambridge: Cambridge University Press, 1994), 114.

4. James Anthony Froude, "England's Forgotten Worthies," in *Short Studies on Great Subjects*, ed. David Ogg (London: Collins, 1963), 153.

5. Thomas Hughes, *Tom Brown's School Days* (London: Macmillan, 1979), 2. See Norman Vance's *The Sinews of the Spirit: The Ideal of Christian Manliness in Victorian Literature and Religious Thought* (Cambridge: Cambridge University Press, 1985), quoted later, for an authoritative treatment of muscular Christianity's main proponents, as well as the second section of chapter 3 in David Newsome's

Victorian World Picture: Perceptions and Introspections in an Age of Change (New Brunswick, NJ: Rutgers University Press, 1997).

6. Geoffrey Sharpless, "Clockwork Education: The Persistence of the Arnoldian Ideal," *Postmodern Culture: An Electronic Journal of Interdisciplinary Criticism* 4 (1994): para. 12 Available at http://muse.jhu.edu/journals/postmodern_culture/v004/4.3sharpless.html. Accessed on 26 August 2005. See also Robert Dingley, "Shades of the Prison House: Discipline and Surveillance in *Tom Brown's School Days*," *Victorian Review* 22 (1996): 1–12. Dingley emphasizes that Rugby's chief purpose by the 1830s was "to educate a new generation of governors and legislators," so that under Arnold, the school developed into a "nursery not only of efficient servants of the state but also of its future masters" (6).

7. Hughes, *Tom Brown*, 115, 114, 116, 90, 114.

8. Ibid., 116.

9. As Dennis Allen has pointed out, for Hughes, "athletic competition . . . is . . . a form of symbolic warfare, a battle over land. War is . . . Hughes's favorite metaphor, one that he relentlessly invokes"; see Allen, "Young England," 121.

10. In fact, Wellington's Eton career ended prematurely when, three years after his father's death in 1781, he was removed from the school by his mother to save money and sent to the academy of equitation in Angers. "It seems odd," Elizabeth Longford comments with regard to this most famous anecdote about Wellington's oracular *mots,* "that an alumnus so lukewarm when young, so indifferent when old, should have paid to his *alma mater* the highest tribute in his power: 'The Battle of Waterloo was won on the playing-fields of Eton.' Of all Wellington's alleged *obiter dicta* this is perhaps the best known. Yet probably he never said or thought anything of the kind"; see Longford, *Wellington: The Years of the Sword* (New York and Evanston, IL: Harper and Row, 1969), 16.

11. Hughes, *Tom Brown*, 52.

12. Anonymous, *The Fourteenth of September: A Martial Dirge* (London: Mary S. Rickerby, 1853), 3.11.9–10.

13. Vance, *Sinews,* 142.

14. Ibid., 149.

15. Quoted in James Anthony Froude, *Thomas Carlyle: A History of His Life in London, 1834–1881,* 2 vols. (London: Longmans, Green, 1884), 2:46.

16. Thomas Carlyle, *On Heroes, Hero-Worship and the Heroic in History* (Lincoln and London: University of Nebraska Press, 1966), 114.

17. Ibid.

18. Ibid., 113.

19. N. Thompson, "Immortal Wellington," 273–74.

20. Landow, *Victorian Types,* 152.

21. See Jane Tompkins, *Sensational Designs: The Cultural Work of American Fiction, 1790–1860* (Oxford and New York: Oxford University Press, 1985), 134.

22. Pears, "Gentleman," 220. Greenhalgh suggests that Wellington's funeral found its *"raison d'être* partly in the translation of Napoleon I's remains to France in 1840, and partly in the widely held fears during the 1840s and early 1850s about

British military unpreparedness in the face of possible invasion from France"; see Greenhalgh, "Funeral," 220.

23. Pears, "Gentleman," 217. And as the recent publication of yet another study of *Napoleon and Wellington* indicates, it continues to be; see Andrew Roberts, *Napoleon and Wellington* (London: Weidenfeld and Nicolson, 2001).

24. Anonymous, *The People's Life of the Duke of Wellington* (London: Richard Bentley, 1852), 18, 21–22.

25. John Strawson, *The Duke and the Emperor: Wellington and Napoleon* (London: Constable, 1994), 13.

26. Ibid., 17.

27. *Scotsman,* 22 September 1852, 2.

28. Karl Marx, "The Eighteenth Brumaire of Louis Bonaparte," in *The Marx-Engels Reader,* ed. Robert C. Tucker (New York: Norton, 1978), 595.

29. Arthur Augustus Rees, *The Death of Wellington and the Resurrection of Napoleon, Being a Lecture, Critical, Historical, and Prophetical* (London: J. Nisbet, 1853), 10.

30. *Punch,* 20 November 1852, 229.

31. Pears, "Gentleman," 218.

32. See Charity, *Events and Their Afterlife,* 7.

33. Englishness and national identity became matters of serious controversy only with the expansion of the British Empire (in which Wellington took an active part in India between 1798 and 1805) and the need to simultaneously incorporate and exclude an increasingly heterogeneous assortment of others. In the words of Ian Baucom, "The trouble with the English is that 'their' history happened overseas," even if most of the English wished to believe "that England was uninvolved, untroubled, unaffected by 'its' empire, and that the history of Englishness, consequently, is an entirely local affair"; see Baucom, *Out of Place: Englishness, Empire, and the Locations of Identity* (Princeton, NJ: Princeton University Press, 1999), 40.

34. *Globe and Traveller* (London), 19 November 1852, 2.

35. Arthur Aspinall, *Politics and the Press, 1780–1850* (London: Macmillan and Gibb, 1949), 312–13.

36. *Times,* 18 September 1852, 4.

37. "Englishness" has received a lot of attention since the mid-1980s. For an excellent representative treatment, see Robert Colls and Philip Dodd, eds., *Englishness: Politics and Culture, 1880–1920* (London: Croom Helm, 1986). Dodd's essay on "Englishness and the National Culture" and D. G. Boyce's "'The Marginal Britons': The Irish" are particularly useful in the context of my own discussion. See also David Morse's *High Victorian Culture* (London: Macmillan, 1993), Baucom's *Out of Place,* and the indispensable collection edited by Eric Hobsbawm and Terence Ranger, *The Invention of Tradition* (Cambridge: Cambridge University Press, 1983).

38. *Times,* 15 September 1852, 4.

39. Marie Atkinson Maurice, *The Patriot Warrior: An Historical Sketch of the Life of the Duke of Wellington, for Young Persons* (London: John Farquhar Shaw, 1853).

40. Morse, *High Victorian Culture,* 47.

41. N. Thompson, *Wellington after Waterloo,* 261.

42. James Stevens Curl, *A Celebration of Death: An Introduction to Some of the Buildings, Monuments, and Settings of Funerary Architecture in the Western European Tradition* (London: B. T. Batsford, 1993), 346.

43. For sales figures and an account of the ways in which the *ILN* benefited from major events such as Wellington's funeral, see Peter W. Sinnema, *Dynamics of the Pictured Page: Representing the Nation in the* Illustrated London News (Aldershot, UK: Ashgate, 1998), introduction and chapter 6.

44. *Illustrated London News,* 20 November 1852, 475; hereafter cited as *ILN.*

45. Pearsall, "Burying the Duke," 371.

46. *Morning Herald* (London), 15 September 1852, 4.

47. Maxwell, *Life,* 1:xvi.

48. Ibid., 2:387, 386, 387.

49. Ibid., 1:xii.

50. Epstein, *Recognizing Biography,* 8.

51. Maxwell, *Life,* 1:8, 21, 374.

52. Mieke Bal, *Narratology: Introduction to the Theory of Narrative* (Toronto: University of Toronto Press, 1985), 63.

53. Carlyle, *On Heroes,* 1.

54. Maxwell, *Life,* 2:331.

55. Carlyle, *On Heroes,* 45.

56. Elisabeth Bronfen and Sarah Webster Goodwin, "Introduction," in *Death and Representation,* eds. Elisabeth Bronfen and Sarah Webster Goodwin (Baltimore, MD: Johns Hopkins University Press, 1993), 14.

57. C. R. Alford, *Wellington's Victories, Divine Deliverance: A Sermon* (London: Wertham and Macintosh, 1852), 3, 5, 6.

58. Maxwell, *Life,* 1:xvi.

59. Ibid.

60. Edmund Gosse, "The Custom of Biography," *Anglo-Saxon Review* 8 (March 1901): 195.

61. *Dictionary of National Biography,* ed. Sidney Lee (London: Smith, Elder, 1900), 62: 95.

62. Ibid.

63. "Turning to authorship in her declining years [Wilson] sent out letters offering to exclude her former clients from her memoirs for a price; 'Publish and be damned!' was the Duke's alleged reply, and certainly he appeared in her account"; see N. Thompson, *Wellington after Waterloo,* 25.

64. As Wilson admitted, dates were not her forte. Readers can assume, however, that her adventures with Wellington occurred sometime between 1809 and 1815, since the duke said his final farewell to Wilson just before he "betook himself again to the wars" in Spain; see Harriette Wilson, *Memoirs* (London: W. Dugdale, 1825), 38. This would make Wellington forty to forty-six years old at the time.

65. Ibid., 14.

66. *Leeds Mercury,* 25 September 1852, 4.

67. Wilson, *Memoirs,* 24, 29.

68. Ibid., 33.

69. Roland Barthes, "Myth Today," in *Mythologies,* trans. Annette Lavers (London: Paladin Grafton, 1989), 118.

70. Ibid., 117, 123.

71. Ibid., 123.

72. Hughes, *Tom Brown,* 74.

73. Barthes, "Myth Today," 123.

74. Dawson, *Soldier Heroes,* 56.

75. Ibid.

Chapter 2: First Rehearsal

1. Thomas Richards, *The Commodity Culture of Victorian England: Advertising and Spectacle, 1851–1914* (New York: Verso, 1990), 17.

2. See, respectively, Tobin Andrews Sparling, *The Great Exhibition: A Question of Taste* (New Haven, CT: Yale Center for British Art, 1982), ix, and Francis Donald Klingender, *Art and the Industrial Revolution* (New York: A. M. Kelley, 1968), 163.

3. *The Great Exhibition: A Facsimile of the Illustrated Catalogue of London's 1851 Crystal Palace Exposition* (New York: Gramercy, 1995), xxiv.

4. Anthony Bird, *Paxton's Palace* (London: Cassell, 1976), 100.

5. "The Great Exhibition was designed less to celebrate Britain's economic successes than to locate and remedy its deficiencies"; see Jeffrey A. Auerbach, *The Great Exhibition of 1851: A Nation on Display* (New Haven, CT: Yale University Press, 1999), 3.

6. The phrase is Richards's; see his *Commodity Culture,* chapter 1.

7. *Bell's Life in London,* 21 November 1852, 3.

8. N. Thompson, "Immortal Wellington," 257.

9. *Fourteenth of September,* 18–19.11.402–8.

10. Richard Glover, *Esdraëlon and Waterloo: A Sermon on the Death of the Duke of Wellington* (London: Hamilton, Adams, 1852), 22.

11. Victoria R. I., *Queen Victoria's Early Letters,* ed. John Raymond (London: B. T. Batsford, 1963), 181–82.

12. *Great Exhibition: A Facsimile,* ix.

13. Ibid., xxiv.

14. Auerbach, *Great Exhibition,* 129.

15. *The Satirist* (London), 16 April 1848, 125.

16. W. R. H. Trowbridge, "Introduction" to *The Letters of the Duke of Wellington to Miss J., 1834–1851,* ed. Christine Terhune Herrick (London: T. Fisher Unwin, 1924), 8.

17. Maxwell, *Life,* 2:370.

18. Wellington Papers, 2/257/106 (hereafter cited as WP). Numerical sequences correspond to the system in use in the Hartley Library's Special Collections, University of Southampton, UK.

19. Charles Babbage, *The Exposition of 1851: Or, Views of the Industry, the Science, and the Government of England* (London: John Murray, 1851), v.

20. Maxwell, *Life,* 2:270.

21. Harriet Arbuthnot, *The Journal of Mrs. Arbuthnot, 1820–1832,* eds. Francis Bamford and the Seventh Duke of Wellington, 2 vols. (London: Macmillan, 1950), 2:417. The stone-throwing incident was documented in one of Wellington's letters to Harriet Arbuthnot: "This morning," the duke noted on 12 October 1831, "a Mob surrounded my House, upon which they commenced an attack with Stones which lasted 50 Minutes in broad daylight before any assistance came. They broke all the Windows on the lower floor [and] . . . a great number in my Room in which I was sitting"; see Arthur Wellesley, *Wellington and His Friends: Letters of the First Duke of Wellington to the Rt. Hon. Charles and Mrs. Arbuthnot, the Earl and Countess of Wilton, Princess Lieven, and Miss Burdett-Coutts* (London: Macmillan, 1965), 99. The subsequent protection of Apsley House's windows with metal shutters led Wellington's detractors to claim that this was the origin of his popular title, Iron Duke.

22. Arbuthnot, *Journal,* 2:421.

23. *ILN,* 25 September 1852, 259.

24. L. Cooper, *Age of Wellington,* xi.

25. Benjamin Disraeli, *Sybil, or, The Two Nations* (Oxford: Oxford University Press, 1991), 23.

26. Bird, *Paxton's Palace,* 76. Ironically, Wellington's visit to the Crystal Palace just before the closing of the exhibition resulted in the singular incident that threatened public order: "The only event that even approached becoming an incident occurred on 7 October, when the Duke of Wellington arrived and was quickly recognized and cheered by the crowds. Those in attendance who could not see the Duke heard the rumble, became alarmed, and cried out that the building was collapsing. The crowd began to panic, there was a huge rush for the doors, and it was all the police could do to carry the Duke to safety"; see Auerbach, *Great Exhibition,* 148.

27. *Great Exhibition: A Facsimile,* xi.

28. Maxwell, *Life,* 2:257.

29. *Morning Chronicle,* 15 September 1852, 4.

30. *ILN,* 14 June 1851, 570.

31. Broadlands Papers, 62 D/13: 17 September 1852. Numerical sequences correspond to the system in use in the Hartley Library's Special Collections, University of Southampton, UK.

32. Margaret Homans, *Royal Representations: Queen Victoria and British Culture, 1837–1876* (Chicago: University of Chicago Press, 1998), 4.

33. Bird, *Paxton's Palace*, 105.

34. Sebastian Evans, *Sonnets on the Death of the Duke of Wellington* (Cambridge: Macmillan, 1852), 3.11.10–12.

35. *Great Exhibition: A Facsimile*, xxiv.

36. Bird, *Paxton's Palace*, 99.

37. *ILN*, 20 November 1852, 475.

38. Michell, *Burial*, 11.36–37.

39. Newsome, *Victorian World Picture*, 122. As Jeffrey Auerbach concludes, "The exhibition confirmed what British manufacturers had suspected for at least a decade, which was that their products were not standing up well to foreign competition"; see Auerbach, *Great Exhibition*, 122.

40. Morley, *Death, Heaven*, 51.

41. Quoted in C. H. Gibbs-Smith, *The Great Exhibition of 1851* (London: Her Majesty's Stationery Office, 1964), 5.

42. *Great Exhibition: A Facsimile*, x, ix.

43. Ibid., viii (my emphasis).

44. Sylvi Johansen, "The Great Exhibition of 1851: A Precipice in Time?" *Victorian Review* 22 (1996): 59.

45. *Great Exhibition: A Facsimile*, viii.

46. Auerbach, *Great Exhibition*, 159.

47. Charles Petrie, *Wellington: A Reassessment* (London: James Barrie, 1956), 256. When William Spicer, a friend of Wellington's longtime confidential servant Christopher Collins, wrote to the latter in September 1852, he not only commented on the "lamentations . . . and mourning already apparent" shortly after the duke's death but also felt compelled to add, "God bless her Majesty and enable her to bear the calamity she has sustained, with submission and health"; see Collins Manuscripts, 69 2/73 (hereafter cited as CollinsMS). Numerical sequences correspond to the system in use in the Hartley Library's Special Collections, University of Southampton, UK.

48. "The Crystal Palace was the first purely rectilinear metal-framed building, without external walls or internal portal bracing, dependent for its lateral stability entirely on rigidly connected vertical columns and light horizontal girders, with a minimum of diagonal bracing in parts of greatest stress by wrought-iron ties. It was, therefore, an entirely new concept"; see Bird, *Paxton's Palace*, 47.

49. *Age*, 25 September 1852, 3.

50. See Fredric Jameson's comments on "'the people' as a kind of general grouping of the poor and 'underprivileged' of all kinds, from which one can recoil in revulsion, but to which one can also, as in some political populisms, nostalgically 'return' to some telluric source of strength," in his *The Political Unconscious* (Ithaca, NY: Cornell University Press, 1981), 189.

51. Richards, *Commodity Culture*, 40.

52. Elizabeth Longford, *Wellington* (London: Weidenfeld and Nicolson, 1992), 25, 501.

Chapter 3: Second Rehearsal

1. An undated memorandum by Christopher Collins mentions a number of such attacks: "The Duke . . . was taken very ill at Apsley House in February 1839 with epileptic fits. The 2nd time at Walmer Castle in November 1839. The 3rd time in Apsley House in February 1840. The 4th time on the 15th of July at Apsley House 1840." See CollinsMS, 69 2/3.

2. Carver Manuscripts, 63 A904/3/23: 4 November 1852 (hereafter cited as CarverMS). Numerical sequences correspond to the system in use in the Hartley Library Special Collections, University of Southampton, UK.

3. Wellesley, *Wellington and Friends*, 271 (12 January 1849).

4. CollinsMS, 69 2/76: 10 October 1852.

5. Morley, *Death, Heaven*, 80.

6. H. Wilson, *Memoirs*, 2:598.

7. *ILN*, 18 September 1852, 215.

8. *Morning Chronicle*, 18 September 1852, 4. The portraitist, T. J. Barker, required significantly more information about Wellington's death than the *ILN*, which produced this full-page, high-quality, and rather imaginative engraving in an extraordinarily short period of time in order to gratify readers' curiosity. Barker wrote to Collins on 25 January 1854 with a series of questions about another "last moments" picture he was undertaking. Clearly, interest in Wellington's passing had not abated more than a year after the fact. "You kindly promised you would give me some information regarding the last moments of the late Duke of Wellington. I am now about to begin the picture, and I should be much obliged if you would answer the following questions: How was the Duke dressed at the time of his death? What *colour* dressing gown? Whether a *pillow* was placed before him? And a *blanket* round his legs?"; see CollinsMS, 69 2/62.

9. *ILN*, 18 September 1852, 226.

10. According to the *ILN*, the watchful figures are those of Lord and Lady Charles Wellesley, Dr. Macarthur, the apothecary Mr. Hulke and his son, the valet Mr. Kendal, and Wellington's butler.

11. *ILN*, 25 September 1852, 263.

12. J. De Kewer Williams, *Iron and Clay: A Funeral Sermon for the Duke of Wellington* (London: John Snow, 1852), 29.

13. Alford, *Wellington's Victories*, 12.

14. *Morning Chronicle*, 19 November 1852, 4.

15. Charles Boutell, *The Hero, and His Example: A Sermon Preached in the Parish Church of Litcham* (London: Whittaker, 1852), 13.

16. Maurice, *Patriot Warrior*, 277.

17. Trowbridge, "Introduction," 13.

18. William Fraser, *Words on Wellington: The Duke—Waterloo—The Ball* (London: John C. Nimmo, 1889), 75.

19. Glover, *Esdraëlon*, 7.

20. Maurice, *Patriot Warrior*, 278.

21. Alfred, Lord Tennyson, *Ode on the Death of the Duke of Wellington* (London: Edward Moxon, 1853), 6.11.28–35.

22. Ibid., 13.11.207–15.

23. *Morning Chronicle* (London), 15 September 1852, 4.

24. *Morning Herald*, 15 September 1852, 4.

25. Benedict Anderson, *Imagined Communities: Reflections on the Origin and Spread of Nationalism* (London and New York: Verso, 1991), 35.

26. *Morning Herald*, 16 September 1852, 4.

27. *Examiner*, 28 September 1852, 593.

28. *Leeds Mercury*, 18 September 1852, 4.

29. Thomas Jackson, *One Star Differing from Another Star in Glory* (London: George Bell, 1852), 9–10.

30. J. Alton Hatchard, *Romanism Overthrown by Wellington: A Sermon* (London: Thomas Hatchard, 1852), 12.

31. Samuel Smiles, *Self-Help, with Illustrations of Character, Conduct, and Perseverance* (Oxford: Oxford University Press, 2002), 195.

32. Charles Edward Kennaway, *The Law of Duty: Or, the Deeds and Difficulties of the Great Duke* (London: J. Whitaker, 1853), 10.

33. Pears, "Gentleman," 225.

34. Wellesley, *Wellington and Friends*, 89 (15 January 1830).

35. N. Thompson, *Wellington after Waterloo*, 14.

36. *Leeds Mercury*, 18 September 1852, 9.

37. Longford, *Years of the Sword*, 19.

38. Patrick Delaforce, *Wellington the Beau: The Life and Loves of the Duke of Wellington* (Moreton-in-Marsh, UK: Windrush, 1990), 29.

39. Joan Wilson, *A Soldier's Wife: Wellington's Marriage* (London: Weidenfeld and Nicolson, 1987), 157.

40. Arbuthnot, *Journal*, 2:5–6 (26 January 1826). Arbuthnot's harsh judgment, however, must be read against a later, somewhat abashed confession. "Excepting my husband and his children," she notes, "I have no feeling of warm interest for any human being but the Duke. There is something about him that fascinates me to a degree that is silly, but which I cannot resist"; see her *Journal*, 2:404 (23 November 1830).

41. Maxwell, *Life*, 2:375.

42. Anonymous, *The Iron Duke: Memoirs of the Duke of Wellington from Authentic Sources* (York, UK: J. Sampson, 1852), 81, 36, 53–54.

43. Longford, *Wellington*, 121–22.

44. Maxwell, *Life*, 2:113.

45. Ibid., 1:56.

46. *Morning Herald*, 15 September 1852, 5.

47. Philip Henry, *Notes of Conversations with the Duke of Wellington, 1831–1851* (London: Humphrey Milford, 1938).

48. *Morning Herald,* 15 September 1852, 4.
49. *Fourteenth of September,* 18.11.398–99.
50. Maxwell, *Life,* 1:xvi.
51. May, *Panegyric,* 31, 33–34.
52. Morley, *Death, Heaven,* 81.

Chapter 4: The Waiting Game

1. *Age,* 2 October 1852, 2.
2. Wolffe, *Great Deaths,* 46.
3. Quoted in Behrendt, *Royal Mourning,* 1.
4. Ibid., 177–78.
5. Ibid., 183.
6. Newsome, *Victorian World Picture,* 155.
7. Christopher Eimer, *Medallic Portraits of the Duke of Wellington* (London: Spink, 1994), 5.
8. Ibid. Eight medals immortalizing Wellington's death are on display in the National Army Museum's (Royal Hospital Road, Chelsea) permanent "Road to Waterloo" exhibition. This display's main attraction, Capt. William Siborne's geographically accurate, three-dimensional, 420-square-foot model of the Battle of Waterloo, capturing the precise moment when Napoleon's Imperial Guard had been repelled in disorder and completed in 1838 with the installation of 75,000 tin-lead soldiers, certainly takes its place among the more remarkable, extant commemorative objects for Wellington.
9. Lord Gerald Wellesley and John Steegman, *The Iconography of the First Duke of Wellington* (London: J. M. Dent and Sons, 1935), ix. The same authors note that, after the Battle of Talavera in July 1809, illustrations of Wellington's victory on the field "reached England and were seized on not only by the print-sellers but also by the potters of Staffordshire and the enamelers of Battersea, the painters of snuff-boxes, the horn-pressers, the pewterers, the turners, the bronze-casters, the medallists, the fan-makers, and the iron-workers" (xv).
10. See John Physick's *The Duke of Wellington in Caricature* (London: Her Majesty's Stationery Office, 1965), for a discussion of forty-four reproduced plates by caricaturists such as Heath, Doyle, and Charles Williams.
11. Ronald Sutherland Gower, *Sir Thomas Lawrence* (London: Goupil, 1900), 111.
12. Natalie M. Houston, "Reading the Victorian Souvenir: Sonnets and Photographs of the Crimean War," *Yale Journal of Criticism* 14, no. 2 (2001): 374.
13. Ibid., 369.
14. *ILN,* 2 July 1842, 127.
15. Ibid., "Preface" to vol. 1 (1842), iv.
16. Ibid., vol. 3.
17. *Morning Herald,* 17 November 1852, 4.

18. Morley, *Death, Heaven,* 85.

19. *Morning Herald,* 17 November 1852, 5.

20. *Scotsman,* 20 November 1852, 3.

21. Ibid., 18 September 1852, 2.

22. Ibid.

23. Morley, *Death, Heaven,* 75. "By the 1840s . . . the case for the reform and simplification of funeral ceremonies had been recognized: it was also recognized that the desire for as grand a funeral as possible would be difficult to eradicate" (27). The passing of the Metropolitan Interments Act in 1850 gave power to the Board of Health to provide cemeteries across the country, closing churchyards and setting fixed charges for burials. "The truth was that the times were changing; although the palmy days of the great funeral were by no means over . . . for the undertakers themselves the knell had begun to toll" (51).

24. Ibid., 88.

25. Ibid.

26. *Age,* 13 November 1852, 5.

27. *Leeds Mercury,* 2 October 1852, 1.

28. Richards, *Commodity Culture,* 88.

29. Margaret Beetham, "Towards a Theory of the Periodical as a Publishing Genre," in *Investigating Victorian Journalism,* ed. Laurel Brake, Aled Jones, and Lionel Madden (Basingstoke, UK: Macmillan, 1990), 26.

30. *Leeds Mercury,* 25 September 1852, 9.

31. *Morning Chronicle,* 20 September 1852, 5.

32. Clare Gittings, *Death, Burial and the Individual in Early Modern England* (London: Routledge, 1984), 232.

33. *Morning Chronicle,* 20 September 1852, 5.

34. Aled Jones, "Local Journalism in Victorian Political Culture," in Brake, Jones, and Madden, *Investigating Victorian Journalism,* 67.

35. Lucy Brown, "The Growth of a National Press," in Brake, Jones, and Madden, *Investigating Victorian Journalism,* 134.

36. Ibid., 133.

37. *Leeds Mercury,* 20 November 1852, 4.

38. *Morning Chronicle,* 19 November 1852, 9.

39. *ILN,* 25 September 1852, 263; 6 November 1852, 392.

40. Ibid., 25 September 1852, 242.

41. Ibid., 20 November 1852, 451.

42. Marie-Christine Leps, *Apprehending the Criminal: The Production of Deviance in Nineteenth-Century Discourse* (Durham, NC: Duke University Press, 1992), 96.

43. Beetham, "Towards a Theory," 28.

44. *Morning Chronicle,* 15 September 1852, 5.

45. Edward Royle, "Newspapers and Periodicals in Historical Research," in Brake, Jones, and Madden, *Investigating Victorian Journalism,* 51.

46. *Times,* 15 September 1852, 4.

47. *John Bull,* 18 September 1852, 600.

48. *Morning Chronicle,* 20 September 1852, 5.

49. Dawson, *Soldier Heroes,* 116.

50. John Scott, *The Vanity of All Earthly Greatness: A Sermon* (Hull, UK: R. T. Cussons, 1852), 25.

51. *Punch,* 18 September 1852, 147, 11.41–42, 45.

52. *ILN,* 2 July 1842, 127.

53. Ibid.

54. *Morning Chronicle,* 15 September 1852, 4.

55. *Leeds Mercury,* 20 November 1852, 4.

56. John Plotz, *The Crowd: British Literature and Public Politics* (Berkeley: University of California Press, 2000), 10.

57. *Times,* 18 November 1852, 4.

58. *Morning Chronicle,* 21 September 1852, 4.

59. *Leeds Mercury,* 20 November 1852, 4.

60. E. P. Thompson, *The Making of the English Working Class* (London: Penguin, 1988), 79.

61. *Morning Chronicle,* 18 September 1852, 4.

62. Victoria, *Early Letters,* 402.

63. Munich, *Queen Victoria's Secrets,* 82.

64. Richards, *Commodity Culture,* 37.

65. *Times,* 19 November 1852, 5.

66. Garlick, "Staging of Death," 63.

67. *ILN,* 20 November 1852, 434.

68. Broadlands Papers, 66 D/13.

69. Maurice, *Patriot Warrior,* 263.

70. CarverMS, 63 45/157: 10 November 1852.

71. *Morning Herald,* 19 November 1852, 4.

Chapter 5: Obsequies and Sanctification

1. Morley, *Death, Heaven,* 83.

2. Jackson, *One Star,* 6.

3. Leopold Ettlinger, "The Duke of Wellington's Funeral Car," *Journal of the Warburg and Courtauld Institutes* 3 (1939–40): 256.

4. Morley, *Death, Heaven,* 83.

5. Ettlinger, "Wellington's Funeral Car," 259.

6. See Garlick, "Staging of Death," 69–70.

7. Garlick does not credit the *Builder,* a specialist journal for architects, engineers, and operatives, for making a similar comparison. "Although there is a certain massive richness about the car, it cannot be pronounced wholly satisfactory," a writer for the *Builder* noted on 20 November 1852: "It strikingly recalls a

railway truck, and no defense can be offered for the half-halberd, half candelabrum character of the supports for the canopy" (731).

8. See also Greenhalgh, who argues that "one of the direct sources for Wellington's funeral carriage is that of Alexander himself, built to carry his body from Babylon to Egypt," in his "Funeral," 222. The connection between Wellington's funeral car and the example of Caesar's triumph over the Gauls is made explicit in Caravita and Liverati's 1815 drama, *Il Trionfo di Cesare Sopra I Galli* (*Cantata as Represented at the King's Theatre* (London: Winchester and Son). Not only is the play dedicated to the "Honour of the Glorious Victory obtained by the Immortal Wellington over the French Army, June 18, 1815," its Chief Augur predicts the coming of Wellington ("'Let us rejoice; the Heavens are propitious to us. . . . It is true that Rome shall fall, but . . . to Britain . . . shall rise . . . a hero sublime, full of immortal glory, of knowledge, and of victory'" [14]), and it concludes with a remarkable tableau: "The scene is gradually illuminated, while is seen descending in the clouds Britannia, who appears rejoicing over her son Wellington, with emblematic devices, while descending, the chorus of 'See the Conquering Hero Comes' is sung" (15).

9. Ettlinger, "Wellington's Funeral Car," 259.

10. *Examiner,* 20 November 1852, 737.

11. Quoted in Philip Guedalla, *The Duke* (London: Hodder and Stoughton, 1931), 476, 451.

12. Charles Greville, *The Greville Memoirs, 1814–1860,* ed. Lytton Strachey and Roger Fulford, 7 vols. (London: Macmillan, 1938), 6:360–61.

13. Ibid., 6:370.

14. Richards, *Commodity Culture,* 31.

15. Thomas Cooper, *The Life of Thomas Cooper* (London: Hodder and Stoughton, 1872), 330, 332.

16. Ibid., 333.

17. Richards, *Commodity Culture,* 4.

18. T. Cooper, *Life,* 333.

19. Ettlinger, "Wellington's Funeral Car," 256.

20. Elizabeth Longford found the former appellation to be so ubiquitous in nineteenth-century sources that she subtitled the second volume of her important Wellington biography *Pillar of State* (to follow *Wellington: Years of the Sword*).

21. *Leeds Mercury,* 25 September 1852, 4.

22. T. Cooper, *Life,* 2.

23. Ibid., 330.

24. *Examiner,* 18 September 1852, 593.

25. Carlyle, *On Heroes,* 1.

26. Greville, *Memoirs,* 6:370.

27. *Times,* 22 November 1852, 5.

28. Morley, *Death, Heaven,* 86.

29. H. Wilson, *Memoirs,* 2:609.

30. Simon Jervis and Maurice Tomlin, *Apsley House: Wellington Museum* (London: Victoria and Albert Museum, 1995), 5.

31. Garlick, "Staging of Death," 59.

32. *ILN*, 22 November 1852, 475.

33. See also John Yarrow's *Monody on the Death of the Duke of Wellington* (London: A. M. Pigott, 1852): "A father's loss our Queen must still deplore, / While she reflects, his wisdom can no more / Counsel in senate, or direct in field, / And wield the sword his mightier arm would wield" (11.37–40).

34. *Times*, 18 November 1852, 5.

35. *Morning Herald*, 19 November 1852, 4.

36. Ibid., 7.

37. *Leeds Mercury*, 20 November 1952, 4.

38. *Morning Herald*, 19 November 1852, 7.

39. *Age*, 13 November 1852, 4.

40. Quoted in *Times*, 19 November 1852, 2.

41. See the appendix to Wolffe's *Great Deaths* for a useful reproduction of the 1852 document, "Precedents of Public Funerals Which May Be Applicable to the Funeral of the Duke of Wellington" (290–93). Here, the different yet overlapping responsibilities of various individuals and institutions is outlined as a potential model for Wellington's obsequies, with special attention paid to the prerogatives of the lord chamberlain, earl marshal, commander in chief, commissioners of works, dean of the cathedral, commissioners of the Metropolitan Police, lord mayor of London, and undertaker.

42. *Examiner*, 20 November 1852, 737.

43. Ibid.

44. Maurice, *Patriot Warrior*, 237.

45. Glover, *Esdraëlon*, i.

46. John Baines, *Honourable Sepulture the Christian's Due: A Sermon* (London: Joseph Martins, 1852), 8.

47. John G. Manly, *A Pulpit Estimate of Wellington* (London: Partridge and Oakey, 1852), 5.

48. H. Wilson, *Memoirs*, 1:142.

49. *The Letters of the Duke of Wellington to Miss J., 1834–1851*, ed. Christine Terhune Herrick (London: T. Fisher Unwin, 1924), 56.

50. Ibid., 88.

51. Ibid., 120 (13 March 1840).

52. Ibid., 128 (n.d.).

53. Dawson, *Soldier Heroes*, 82. Dawson notes that "the years 1854–65 saw the notion of 'the Christian soldier' gain widespread currency beyond narrowly evangelical circles, in a movement promoting conversion among the ranks and the moral reform of the Army" (81).

54. Williams, *Iron and Clay*, 3, 24.

55. Ibid., 26.

56. Wellesley, *Wellington and Friends,* 279.

57. Dawson, *Soldier Heroes,* 62, 83.

58. Wolffe, *Great Deaths,* 65.

59. John Hayden, *Wellington: His Character and Actions* (London: Jackson and Walford, 1853), 19, 20, 20–21.

60. Close, *National Obsequies,* 17.

61. Delaforce, *Wellington the Beau,* 25.

62. Close, *National Obsequies,* 14.

63. Scott, *Vanity,* 6.

64. Elisabeth Bronfen, *Over Her Dead Body: Death, Femininity and the Aesthetic* (New York: Routledge, 1992), xi.

65. Scott, *Vanity,* 18, 8.

66. *Morning Chronicle,* 19 November 1852, 4.

Chapter 6: Irish Opposition

1. Garlick, "Staging of Death," 75.

2. Longford, *Years of the Sword,* 156.

3. Evans, *Sonnets,* 1.11.10–11.

4. *Galway Vindicator,* 18 September 1852, 2.

5. John Murray, *Wellington: The Place and Day of His Birth Ascertained and Demonstrated* (Dublin: Dublin University Press, 1852), 14.

6. See Longford, *Years of the Sword,* 5.

7. *John Bull,* 18 September 1852, 601.

8. Longford, *Wellington,* 13.

9. *Belfast Mercury,* 18 September 1852, 2.

10. *Times,* 15 September 1852, 4.

11. *Belfast Mercury,* 9 October 1852, 2.

12. Ibid., 21 September 1852, 2.

13. *Times,* 22 September 1852, 4.

14. *Freeman's Journal,* 17 September 1852, 2.

15. *Galway Vindicator,* 18 September 1852, 2.

16. *Times,* 29 September 1852, 4.

17. Ibid., 27 September 1852, 4.

18. Ibid., 29 September 1852, 4.

19. *Belfast Mercury,* 9 October 1852, 2.

20. *Freeman's Journal,* 17 September 1852, 2.

21. Luke Gibbons, "Race against Time: Racial Discourse and Irish History," *Oxford Literary Review* 13, nos. 1–2 (1991): 105.

22. Prys Morgan, "The Hunt for the Welsh Past in the Romantic Period," in *The Invention of Tradition,* ed. Eric Hobsbawm and Terence Ranger (Cambridge: Cambridge University Press, 1983), 68–69.

23. *Freeman's Journal*, 18 November 1852, 2.

24. Michell, *Burial*, 11.40–42.

25. *Freeman's Journal*, 16 September 1852, 2.

26. *Galway Vindicator*, 18 September 1852, 2. Sir Robert Peel had died in 1850.

27. *Age*, 25 September 1852, 4.

28. Hatchard, *Romanism Overthrown*, 28–29.

29. Dawson, *Soldier Heroes*, 26.

30. Declan Kiberd, *Inventing Ireland* (Cambridge, MA: Harvard University Press, 1995), 115.

31. As Christopher Morash has pointed out, "In the case of the Famine, it is the event itself which eludes definition. There is no single, clear consensus as to what constituted the Famine. For Charles Trevelyan, the Famine coincided with the government relief effort; hence, when the relief effort ceased, so too did the Famine"; see Morash, *Writing the Irish Famine* (Oxford: Clarendon, 1995), 1–2.

32. Peter Gray, *The Irish Famine* (London: Thames and Hudson, 1995), 110. See also Christine Kinealy's *A Death-Dealing Famine: The Great Hunger in Ireland* (London: Pluto, 1997): "The suffering of the Irish was initially greeted with sympathy . . . [but] as thousands of diseased paupers landed in Britain, threatening public health, taxes and the jobs of the working classes, opinion was increasingly motivated by fear and hostility" (131).

33. Kiberd, *Inventing Ireland*, 30. "By [Matthew] Arnold's day," Kiberd notes, this image "had been well and truly formed."

34. Gibbons, "Race against Time," 98.

35. P. Gray, "Wellington and the Government of Ireland, 1832–46," in Woolgar, *Wellington Studies III*, 221.

36. Kennaway, *Law of Duty*, 27.

37. Catherine Hall, *White, Male and Middle-Class: Explorations in Feminism and History* (Cambridge: Polity, 1992), 26.

38. John S. Rickard, "Introduction" to *Irishness and (Post)Modernism*, ed. John S. Rickard (Lewisburg, PA: Bucknell University Press, 1994), 15.

39. Gray, "Wellington and the Government of Ireland," 203–4.

40. *Freeman's Journal*, 16 September 1852, 2.

41. *Times*, 15 September 1852, 4.

42. J. Wilson, *A Soldier's Wife*, 101.

43. Gray, "Wellington and the Government of Ireland," 204.

44. Arthur Wellesley, *The Speeches of the Duke of Wellington in Parliament*, ed. Colonel Gurwood, 2 vols. (London: John Murray, 1852), 1:109. This is an extract from a speech of 9 February 1822.

45. Longford, *Wellington*, 378.

46. Gray, "Wellington and the Government of Ireland," 203.

47. *Galway Vindicator*, 18 September 1852, 2.

48. *Age*, 2 October 1852, 4.

49. *Belfast Mercury*, 9 October 1852, 2.

50. R. J. Donne, *The Example of the Duke of Wellington: A Sermon, Preached at the Commemoration of the Birthday of the Duke of Wellington* (London: Bell and Daldy, 1860), 8.

51. *Age,* 2 October 1852, 4.

52. Kiberd, *Inventing Ireland,* 8.

53. Ibid., 13.

54. Ibid., 30.

55. Ibid.

56. *Morning Herald,* 18 September 1852, 4.

57. *John Bull,* 25 September 1852, 616–17.

58. *Galway Vindicator,* 18 September 1852, 2.

59. Ibid., 20 November 1852, 2.

60. Ibid., 29 September 1852, 2.

61. *Morning Chronicle,* 19 November 1852, 4.

62. Goodwin and Bronfen, "Introduction," 9.

63. Ibid., 7.

64. *Punch,* vol. 23 (1852), 147.

65. Ibid., vol. 15 (1848), 146.

66. Ibid.

Chapter 7: Epilogue

1. With a girth of twenty-two feet and eight inches, Copenhagen's belly was large enough to host in comfort several of the sculptor's friends for a celebratory supper before the work was bolted into place. As a result of its size, Wyatt's Wellington was occasionally satirized as an anachronism, a Rhodian Colossus for nineteenth-century London. A rider on horseback could readily pass under Copenhagen's torso without danger of scraping his beaver hat.

2. F. Darrell Munsell, *The Victorian Controversy Surrounding the Wellington War Memorial* (Lewiston, NY: Edwin Mellen, 1991), 103.

3. As a number of subsequent references indicate, the controversy has been partially documented by scholars such as F. D. Munsell, John Physick, and Alison Yarrington. Their focus, however, is limited to the statue's unpopularity as a fascinating case in which a "delicate mixture of artistic aspiration and public understanding curdled"; see Yarrington, *His Achilles Heel? Wellington and Public Art* (Southampton, UK: University of Southampton Press, 1998), 33.

4. William Makepeace Thackeray, *Vanity Fair,* eds. Geoffrey and Kathleen Tillotson (Boston: Houghton Mifflin, 1963), 206, 80.

5. Mary Hammond, "History and War in *Vanity Fair,*" *Literature and History* 11 (2002): 29.

6. John Hagan, "A Note on the Napoleonic Background of *Vanity Fair,*" *Nineteenth-Century Fiction* 15 (1961): 360.

7. John Physick, *The Wellington Monument* (London: Her Majesty's Stationery Office, 1970), 2.

8. See the eighth chapter of Finley's *Angel in the Sun: Turner's Vision of History* (Montreal and Kingston, Canada: McGill-Queen's University Press, 1999), for a brief history of industrial activity as an influence on eighteenth- and early nineteenth-century visual art.

9. Immanuel Kant, *The Critique of Judgement*, trans. James Creed Meredith (Oxford: Clarendon, 1988), 92.

10. Ibid., 103. See also the *Critique*, bk. 2: "If we are to give a suitable example of [the sublime] for the Critique of *aesthetic* judgment, we must not point to the sublime in works of art, e.g. buildings, statues and the like, where a human end determines the form as well as the magnitude, nor yet in things of nature, *that in their very concept import a definite end*, e.g. animals of a recognized natural order, but in rude nature merely as involving magnitude" (100).

11. Physick, *Wellington Monument*, 7.

12. Kant, *Critique*, 97.

13. *The People's Life*, 8.

14. Physick, *Wellington Monument*, 10.

15. Quoted in ibid.

16. Richards, *Commodity Culture*, 54.

17. Indeed, Wellington declared himself "dead" to much of the proceedings, leaving London for Walmer Castle while the statue was transported past Apsley House on its way to the arch.

18. Richards, *Commodity Culture*, 56.

19. In fact, public anticipation was acute for nearly three years. According to Physick, "There was . . . a halt in casting, during January 1843, due to a shortage of metal. From about this time onwards London read about, and waited for, the great day when the statue would be revealed"; see Physick, *Wellington Monument*, 7.

20. *ILN*, 14 May 1842, 1.

21. Physick, *Wellington Monument*, 10.

22. *Punch*, vol. 11 (1846), 146.

23. Ibid., 144.

24. Ibid., 41.

25. Asa Briggs and Susan Briggs, "Preface" to *Cap and Bell: Punch's Chronicle of English History in the Making, 1841–1861* (London: Macdonald, 1972), xvii.

26. See ibid.: "*Punch* . . . was very much a metropolitan paper. . . . These were the golden years of the provincial press, yet *Punch* visited the provinces only on holiday or for the sake of a laugh. . . . The problems which preoccupied it even during its most radical phases were London problems" (xxix).

27. Physick, *Wellington Monument*, 7.

28. Anonymous, *Reflections in Rhyme, on the Wellington Memorial and the Column of Napoleon* (London: Ridgeways, 1839), ll.117–22.

29. Victoria, *Early Letters*, 127.

30. Ibid., 129.

31. Ibid., 130–31.

32. Quoted in Benedict Read, *Victorian Sculpture* (New Haven, CT: Yale University Press, 1982), 15.

33. *Builder,* 10 October 1846, 484.

34. Quoted in Read, *Victorian Sculpture,* 19.

35. S. G. P. Ward, *Wellington* (London: B. T. Batsford, 1963), 121, 127, 130.

36. Yarrington, *Achilles Heel,* 33.

37. By midcentury, London had paid ample tribute to Wellington in the way of public memorials: "The walls of official buildings, clubs, and private houses were adorned with iconic portraits and busts for which [Wellington] was never loath to sit. Wherever he went in the capital at least, it was difficult to avoid evidence that he was the nation's household god"; see N. Thompson, *Wellington after Waterloo,* 8.

38. Smiles, *Self-Help,* 234.

39. Yarrington, *Achilles Heel,* 13.

40. Smiles, *Self-Help,* 221.

41. Ibid., 235, 236.

42. Ibid., 235 (my emphasis).

43. Henry Thomas Braithwaite, *Ode on the Death of the Duke of Wellington* (London: William Pickering, 1852), ll.71, 162–70.

44. *London Review and Weekly Journal of Politics, Art, and Society* 2 (1 September 1860): 201.

45. Greville, *Memoirs,* 6:360–61.

46. Finley, *Angel,* 107.

47. J. Hillis Miller, *Illustration* (Cambridge, MA: Harvard University Press, 1992), 130.

48. Ibid., 131, 135.

49. Finley, *Angel,* 106.

50. Edmund Burke, *A Philosophical Enquiry into the Origin of Our Ideas of the Sublime and Beautiful,* ed. James T. Boulton (Notre Dame, IN: University of Notre Dame Press, 1968), 80.

51. Kant, *Critique,* 100.

52. See, respectively, Dawson, *Soldier Heroes,* 147, 145.

53. Ibid., 121.

54. Arthur Bryant, *The Great Duke* (New York: William Morrow, 1972), 11.

BIBLIOGRAPHY

Periodicals

The Age (London)
Belfast Mercury
Bell's Life in London (London)
The Builder (London)
Examiner (London)
Freeman's Journal (Dublin)
Galway Vindicator
Globe and Traveller (London)
Illustrated London News (*ILN*)
John Bull (London)
Leeds Mercury
London Review and Weekly Journal of Politics, Art, and Society
Morning Chronicle (London)
Morning Herald (London)
Punch (London)
Satirist (London)
Scotsman (Edinburgh)
Times (London)

Manuscripts

Broadlands Papers. 62 D/13. Hartley Library, Special Collections, University of Southampton, UK.

Carver Manuscripts. Hartley Library, Special Collections, University of Southampton, UK.

Collins Manuscripts. Hartley Library, Special Collections, University of Southampton, UK.

Wellington Papers. Hartley Library, Special Collections, University of Southampton, UK.

Books and Articles

Alford, C. R. *Wellington's Victories, Divine Deliverance: A Sermon.* London: Wertham and Macintosh, 1852.

Allen, Dennis W. "Young England: Muscular Christianity and the Politics of the Body in *Tom Brown's School Days*." In *Muscular Christianity: Embodying the Victorian Age,* ed. Donald E. Hall. Cambridge: Cambridge University Press, 1994.

Anderson, Benedict. *Imagined Communities: Reflections on the Origin and Spread of Nationalism.* London and New York: Verso, 1991.

Arbuthnot, Harriet. *The Journal of Mrs. Arbuthnot, 1820–1832.* Ed. Francis Bamford and the Seventh Duke of Wellington. 2 vols. London: Macmillan, 1950.

Aspinall, Arthur. *Politics and the Press, 1780–1850.* London: Macmillan and Gibb, 1949.

Auerbach, Jeffrey A. *The Great Exhibition of 1851: A Nation on Display.* New Haven, CT: Yale University Press, 1999.

Babbage, Charles. *The Exposition of 1851: Or, Views of the Industry, the Science, and the Government of England.* London: John Murray, 1851.

Baines, John. *Honourable Sepulture the Christian's Due: A Sermon.* London: Joseph Martins, 1852.

Bal, Mieke. *Narratology: Introduction to the Theory of Narrative.* Toronto: University of Toronto Press, 1985.

Barthes, Roland. "Myth Today." In *Mythologies,* by Roland Barthes. Trans. Annette Lavers. London: Paladin Grafton, 1989.

Baucom, Ian. *Out of Place: Englishness, Empire, and the Locations of Identity.* Princeton, NJ: Princeton University Press, 1999.

Beetham, Margaret. "Towards a Theory of the Periodical as a Publishing Genre." In Brake, Jones, and Madden, *Investigating Victorian Journalism.*

Behrendt, Stephen C. *Royal Mourning and Regency Culture: Elegies and Memorials of Princess Charlotte.* Houndmills, UK: Macmillan, 1997.

Bird, Anthony. *Paxton's Palace.* London: Cassell, 1976.

Boutell, Charles. *The Hero, and His Example: A Sermon Preached in the Parish Church of Litcham.* London: Whittaker, 1852.

Braithwaite, Henry Thomas. *Ode on the Death of the Duke of Wellington.* London: William Pickering, 1852.

Brake, Laurel, Aled Jones, and Lionel Madden, eds. *Investigating Victorian Journalism.* Basingstoke, UK: Macmillan, 1990.

Briggs, Asa, and Susan Briggs. "Preface." In *Cap and Bell:* Punch's *Chronicle of English History in the Making, 1841–1861,* ed. Asa and Susan Briggs. London: Macdonald, 1972.

Bronfen, Elisabeth. *Over Her Dead Body: Death, Femininity and the Aesthetic.* New York: Routledge, 1992.

Bronfen, Elisabeth, and Sarah Webster Goodwin. "Introduction." In *Death and Representation,* ed. Elisabeth Bronfen and Sarah Webster Goodwin. Baltimore, MD: Johns Hopkins University Press, 1993.

Brown, Lucy. "The Growth of a National Press." In Brake, Jones, and Madden, *Investigating Victorian Journalism.*

Bryant, Arthur. *The Great Duke.* New York: William Morrow, 1972.

Burke, Edmund. *A Philosophical Enquiry into the Origin of Our Ideas of the Sublime and Beautiful.* Ed. James T. Boulton. Notre Dame, IN: University of Notre Dame Press, 1968.

Caravita, Signor, and Signor Liverati. *Il Trionfo di Cesare Sopra I Galli (Cantata as Represented at the King's Theatre).* London: Winchester and Son, 1815.

Carlyle, Thomas. *On Heroes, Hero-Worship and the Heroic in History.* Lincoln and London: University of Nebraska Press, 1966.

Charity, A. C. *Events and Their Afterlife: The Dialectics of Christian Typology in the Bible and Dante.* Cambridge: Cambridge University Press, 1966.

Close, A. M. *National Obsequies Sanctioned by Holy Writ. A Sermon.* London: Hatchard, 1852.

Colls, Robert, and Philip Dodd, eds. *Englishness: Politics and Culture, 1880–1920.* London: Croom Helm, 1986.

Conder, G. W. *Duty and Destiny, or, the Ruling Ideas of Wellington and Napoleon.* London: Hamilton, Adams, 1852.

Cooper, Leonard. *The Age of Wellington: The Life and Times of the Duke of Wellington, 1769–1852.* London: Macmillan, 1964.

Cooper, Thomas. *The Life of Thomas Cooper.* London: Hodder and Stoughton, 1872.

Curl, James Stevens. *A Celebration of Death: An Introduction to Some of the Buildings, Monuments, and Settings of Funerary Architecture in the Western European Tradition.* London: B. T. Batsford, 1993.

Dawson, Graham. *Soldier Heroes: British Adventure, Empire and the Imagining of Masculinities.* London: Routledge, 1994.

Delaforce, Patrick. *Wellington the Beau: The Life and Loves of the Duke of Wellington.* Moreton-in-Marsh, UK: Windrush, 1990.

Dictionary of National Biography. Ed. Sidney Lee. London: Smith, Elder, 1900.

Dingley, Robert. "Shades of the Prison House: Discipline and Surveillance in *Tom Brown's School Days.*" *Victorian Review* 22 (1996): 1–12.

Disraeli, Benjamin. *Sybil, or, The Two Nations.* Oxford: Oxford University Press, 1991.

Donne, R. J. *The Example of the Duke of Wellington: A Sermon, Preached at the Commemoration of the Birthday of the Duke of Wellington.* London: Bell and Daldy, 1860.

Eimer, Christopher. *Medallic Portraits of the Duke of Wellington.* London: Spink, 1994.

Epstein, William H. *Recognizing Biography.* Philadelphia: University of Pennsylvania Press, 1987.

Ettlinger, Leopold. "The Duke of Wellington's Funeral Car." *Journal of the Warburg and Courtauld Institutes* 3 (1939–40): 254–59.

Evans, Sebastian. *Sonnets on the Death of the Duke of Wellington.* Cambridge: Macmillan, 1852.

Finley, Gerald. *Angel in the Sun: Turner's Vision of History.* Montreal and Kingston: McGill-Queen's University Press, 1999.

The Fourteenth of September: A Martial Dirge. London: Mary S. Rickerby, 1853.

Fraser, William. *Words on Wellington: The Duke—Waterloo—The Ball.* London: John C. Nimmo, 1889.

Froude, James Anthony. "England's Forgotten Worthies." In *Short Studies on Great Subjects,* ed. David Ogg. London: Collins, 1963.

———. *Thomas Carlyle: A History of His Life in London, 1834–1881.* 2 vols. London: Longmans, Green, 1884.

Garlick, Harry. "The Staging of Death: Iconography and the State Funeral of the Duke of Wellington." *Australian Journal of Art* 9 (1991): 58–77.

Gibbons, Luke. "Race against Time: Racial Discourse and Irish History." *Oxford Literary Review* 13, nos. 1–2 (1991): 105.

Gibbs-Smith, C. H. *The Great Exhibition of 1851.* London: Her Majesty's Stationery Office, 1964.

Gittings, Clare. *Death, Burial and the Individual in Early Modern England.* London: Routledge, 1984.

Glavin, John. *After Dickens: Reading, Adaptation and Performance.* Cambridge: Cambridge University Press, 1999.

Glover, Richard. *Esdraëlon and Waterloo: A Sermon on the Death of the Duke of Wellington.* London: Hamilton, Adams, 1852.

Gosse, Edmund. "The Custom of Biography." *Anglo-Saxon Review* 8 (March 1901): 195–208.

Gower, Ronald Sutherland. *Sir Thomas Lawrence.* London: Goupil, 1900.

Gray, P. "Wellington and the Government of Ireland, 1832–46." In Woolgar, *Wellington Studies III.*

Gray, Peter. *The Irish Famine.* London: Thames and Hudson, 1995.

The Great Exhibition: A Facsimile of the Illustrated Catalogue of London's 1851 Crystal Palace Exposition. New York: Gramercy, 1995.

Greenhalgh, Michael. "The Funeral of the Duke of Wellington." *Apollo* 98 (September 1973): 220–26.

Greville, Charles. *The Greville Memoirs, 1814–1860.* Ed. Lytton Strachey and Roger Fulford. 7 vols. London: Macmillan, 1938.

Guedalla, Philip. *The Duke.* London: Hodder and Stoughton, 1931.

Hagan, John. "A Note on the Napoleonic Background of *Vanity Fair.*" *Nineteenth-Century Fiction* 15 (1961): 360.

Hall, Catherine. *White, Male and Middle-Class: Explorations in Feminism and History.* Cambridge: Polity, 1992.

Hammond, Mary. "History and War in *Vanity Fair.*" *Literature and History* 11 (2002): 29.

Hatchard, J. Alton. *Romanism Overthrown by Wellington: A Sermon.* London: Thomas Hatchard, 1852.

Hayden, John. *Wellington: His Character and Actions.* London: Jackson and Walford, 1853.

Henry, Philip. *Notes of Conversations with the Duke of Wellington, 1831–1851.* London: Humphrey Milford, 1938.

Hobsbawm, Eric, and Terence Ranger, eds. *The Invention of Tradition.* Cambridge: Cambridge University Press, 1983.

Homans, Margaret. *Royal Representations: Queen Victoria and British Culture, 1837–1876.* Chicago: University of Chicago Press, 1998.

Houlbrooke, Ralph, ed. *Death, Ritual, and Bereavement.* London: Routledge, 1989.

Houston, Gail Turley. *Royalties: The Queen and Victorian Writers.* Charlottesville and London: University Press of Virginia, 1999.

Houston, Natalie M. "Reading the Victorian Souvenir: Sonnets and Photographs of the Crimean War." *Yale Journal of Criticism* 14, no. 2 (2001): 353–83.

Hughes, Thomas. *Tom Brown's School Days.* London: Macmillan, 1979.

The Iron Duke: Memoirs of the Duke of Wellington from Authentic Sources. York, UK: J. Sampson, 1852.

Jackson, Thomas. *One Star Differing from Another Star in Glory.* London: George Bell, 1852.

Jalland, Pat. "Death, Grief, and Mourning in the Upper-Class Family, 1860–1914." In Houlbrooke, *Death, Ritual, and Bereavement.*

Jameson, Fredric. *The Political Unconscious.* Ithaca, NY: Cornell University Press, 1981.

Jervis, Simon, and Maurice Tomlin. *Apsley House: Wellington Museum.* London: Victoria and Albert Museum, 1995.

Johansen, Sylvi. "The Great Exhibition of 1851: A Precipice in Time?" *Victorian Review* 22 (1996): 59–64.

Jones, Aled. "Local Journalism in Victorian Political Culture." In Brake, Jones, and Madden, *Investigating Victorian Journalism.*

Kant, Immanuel. *The Critique of Judgement.* Trans. James Creed Meredith. Oxford: Clarendon, 1988.

Kennaway, Charles Edward. *The Law of Duty: Or, the Deeds and Difficulties of the Great Duke.* London: J. Whitaker, 1853.

Kestner, Joseph A. *Masculinities in Victorian Painting.* Aldershot, UK: Scolar, 1995.

Kiberd, Declan. *Inventing Ireland.* Cambridge, MA: Harvard University Press, 1995.

Kinealy, Christine. *A Death-Dealing Famine: The Great Hunger in Ireland.* London: Pluto, 1997.

Klingender, Francis Donald. *Art and the Industrial Revolution.* New York: A. M. Kelley, 1968.

Landow, George P. *Victorian Types, Victorian Shadows: Biblical Typology in Victorian Literature, Art, and Thought.* Boston and London: Routledge and Kegan Paul, 1980.

Leps, Marie-Christine. *Apprehending the Criminal: The Production of Deviance in Nineteenth-Century Discourse.* Durham, NC: Duke University Press, 1992.

Llewellyn, Nigel. *The Art of Death: Visual Culture in the English Death Ritual, 1500–1800.* London: Reaktion, 1991.

Longford, Elizabeth. *Victoria R. I.* London: Pan, 1964.

———. *Wellington.* London: Weidenfeld and Nicolson, 1992.

———. *Wellington: The Years of the Sword.* New York and Evanston, IL: Harper and Row, 1969.

Manly, John G. *A Pulpit Estimate of Wellington.* London: Partridge and Oakey, 1852.

Marcus, Laura. *Auto-biographical Discourses: Theory, Criticism, Practice.* Manchester, UK: Manchester University Press, 1994.

Marx, Karl. "The Eighteenth Brumaire of Louis Bonaparte." In *The Marx-Engels Reader,* ed. Robert C. Tucker. New York: Norton, 1978.

Maurice, Marie Atkinson. *The Patriot Warrior: An Historical Sketch of the Life of the Duke of Wellington, for Young Persons.* London: John Farquhar Shaw, 1853.

Maxwell, Herbert. *The Life of Wellington: The Restoration of the Martial Power of Great Britain.* 2nd ed. 2 vols. London: Sampson Low, Marston and Co., 1900.

May, Walter B. *A Panegyric in Honour of the Duke of Wellington.* Taunton, UK: Frederick May, 1854.

Metcalf, Peter, and Richard Huntington. *Celebrations of Death: The Anthropology of Mourning Ritual.* Cambridge: Cambridge University Press, 1991.

Michell, Nicholas. *The Burial of Wellington: An Elegiac and Tributary Poem.* London: William Tegg, 1852.

Miller, J. Hillis. *Illustration.* Cambridge, MA: Harvard University Press, 1992.

Morash, Christopher. *Writing the Irish Famine.* Oxford: Clarendon, 1995.

Morey, George. *The True Book about Wellington.* London: Frederick Muller, 1967.

Morgan, Prys. "The Hunt for the Welsh Past in the Romantic Period." In *The Invention of Tradition,* ed. Eric Hobsbawm and Terence Ranger. Cambridge: Cambridge University Press, 1983.

Morley, John. *Death, Heaven and the Victorians.* Pittsburgh, PA: University of Pittsburgh Press, 1971.

Morse, David. *High Victorian Culture.* London: Macmillan, 1993.

Munich, Adrienne. *Queen Victoria's Secrets.* New York: Columbia University Press, 1996.

Munsell, F. Darrell. *The Victorian Controversy Surrounding the Wellington War Memorial.* Lewiston, NY: Edwin Mellen, 1991.

Murray, John. *Wellington: The Place and Day of His Birth Ascertained and Demonstrated.* Dublin: Dublin University Press, 1852.

Newsome, David. *The Victorian World Picture: Perceptions and Introspections in an Age of Change.* New Brunswick, NJ: Rutgers University Press, 1997.

Pears, Iain. "The Gentleman and the Hero: Wellington and Napoleon in the Nineteenth Century." In *Myths of the English,* ed. Roy Porter. Cambridge: Polity, 1992.

Pearsall, Cornelia D. J. "Burying the Duke: Victorian Mourning and the Funeral of the Duke of Wellington." *Victorian Literature and Culture* 27, no. 2 (1999): 377–78.

The People's Life of the Duke of Wellington. London: Richard Bentley, 1852.

Petrie, Charles. *Wellington: A Reassessment.* London: James Barrie, 1956.

Physick, John. *The Duke of Wellington in Caricature.* London: Her Majesty's Stationery Office, 1965.

———. *The Wellington Monument.* London: Her Majesty's Stationery Office, 1970.

Plotz, John. *The Crowd: British Literature and Public Politics.* Berkeley: University of California Press, 2000.

Read, Benedict. *Victorian Sculpture.* New Haven, CT: Yale University Press, 1982.

Rees, Arthur Augustus. *The Death of Wellington and the Resurrection of Napoleon, Being a Lecture, Critical, Historical, and Prophetical.* London: J. Nisbet, 1853.

Reflections in Rhyme, on the Wellington Memorial and the Column of Napoleon. London: Ridgeways, 1839.

Richardson, Ruth. "Why Was Death So Big in Victorian Britain?" In Houlbrooke, *Death, Ritual, and Bereavement.*

Richards, Thomas. *The Commodity Culture of Victorian England: Advertising and Spectacle, 1851–1914.* New York: Verso, 1990.

Rickard, John S. "Introduction." In *Irishness and (Post)Modernism,* ed. John S. Rickard. Lewisburg, PA: Bucknell University Press, 1994.

Roberts, Andrew. *Napoleon and Wellington.* London: Weidenfeld and Nicolson, 2001.

Royle, Edward. "Newspapers and Periodicals in Historical Research." In Brake, Jones, and Madden, *Investigating Victorian Journalism.*

Scott, John. *The Vanity of All Earthly Greatness: A Sermon.* Hull, UK: R. T. Cussons, 1852.

Sharpless, Geoffrey. "Clockwork Education: The Persistence of the Arnoldian Ideal." *Postmodern Culture: An Electronic Journal of Interdisciplinary Criticism* 4 (1994): para 12. Available at http://muse.jhu.edu/journals/postmodern_culture/v004/4.3sharpless.html. Accessed on 25 August 2005.

Sinnema, Peter W. *Dynamics of the Pictured Page: Representing the Nation in the* Illustrated London News. Aldershot, UK: Ashgate, 1998.

Smiles, Samuel. *Self-Help, with Illustrations of Character, Conduct, and Perseverance.* Oxford: Oxford University Press, 2002.

Sparling, Tobin Andrews. *The Great Exhibition: A Question of Taste.* New Haven, CT: Yale Center for British Art, 1982.

Stannard, Martin. "The Necrophiliac Art?" In *The Literary Biography: Problems and Solutions,* ed. Dale Salwak. Iowa City: University of Iowa Press, 1996.

Strawson, John. *The Duke and the Emperor: Wellington and Napoleon.* London: Constable, 1994.

Sussman, Herbert. *Victorian Masculinities: Manhood and Masculine Poetics in Early Victorian Literature and Art.* Cambridge: Cambridge University Press, 1995.

Tennyson, Alfred. *Ode on the Death of the Duke of Wellington.* London: Edward Moxon, 1853.

Thackeray, William Makepeace. *Vanity Fair.* Boston: Houghton Mifflin, 1963.

Thompson, E. P. *The Making of the English Working Class.* London: Penguin, 1988.

Thompson, Neville. "Immortal Wellington: Literary Tributes to the Hero." In Woolgar, *Wellington Studies III.*

———. *Wellington after Waterloo.* London: Routledge and Kegan Paul, 1986.

Tompkins, Jane. *Sensational Designs: The Cultural Work of American Fiction, 1790–1860.* Oxford and New York: Oxford University Press, 1985.

Trowbridge, W. R. H. "Introduction." In *The Letters of the Duke of Wellington to Miss. J., 1834–1851,* ed. Christine Terhune Herrick. London: T. Fisher Unwin, 1924.

Turner, Frank. *Contesting Cultural Authority: Essays in Victorian Intellectual Life.* Cambridge: Cambridge University Press, 1993.

Vance, Norman. *The Sinews of the Spirit: The Ideal of Christian Manliness in Victorian Literature and Religious Thought.* Cambridge: Cambridge University Press, 1985.

Victoria R. I. *Queen Victoria's Early Letters.* Ed. John Raymond. London: B. T. Batsford, 1963.

Ward, S. G. P. *Wellington.* London: B. T. Batsford, 1963.

Wellesley, Arthur. *The Letters of the Duke of Wellington to Miss J., 1834–1851.* Ed. Christine Terhune Merrick. London: T. Fisher Unwin, 1924.

———. *The Speeches of the Duke of Wellington in Parliament.* Ed. Colonel Gurwood. London: John Murray, 1852.

———. *Wellington and His Friends: Letters of the First Duke of Wellington to the Rt. Hon. Charles and Mrs. Arbuthnot, the Earl and Countess of Wilton, Princess Lieven, and Miss Burdett-Coutts.* Ed. Seventh Duke of Wellington. London: Macmillan, 1965.

Wellesley, Lord Gerald, and John Steegman. *The Iconography of the First Duke of Wellington.* London: J. M. Dent and Sons, 1935.

Williams, J. De Kewer. *Iron and Clay: A Funeral Sermon for the Duke of Wellington.* London: John Snow, 1852.

Wilson, Harriette. *Memoirs.* London: W. Dugdale, 1825.

Wilson, Joan. *A Soldier's Wife: Wellington's Marriage.* London: Weidenfeld and Nicolson, 1987.

Wilson, John Marius. *A Memoir of Field-Marshal the Duke of Wellington: With Interspersed Notices of His Principal Associates in Council, and Companions and Opponents in Arms.* 2 vols. London: A. Fullerton, n.d.

Wolffe, John. *Great Deaths: Grieving, Religion, and Nationhood in Victorian and Edwardian Britain.* Oxford: Oxford University Press, 2000.

Woolgar, C. M., ed. *Wellington Studies III.* Southampton, UK: Hartley Institute, 1999.

Yarrington, Alison. *His Achilles Heel? Wellington and Public Art.* Southampton, UK: University of Southampton Press, 1998.

Yarrow, John. *Monody on the Death of the Duke of Wellington.* London: A. M. Pigott, 1852.

INDEX